Critical Acclaim for:
Growing Up Irish Catholic,
and Surviving My Mom's Eleven Sisters

Pat, I think your stuff is hilarious . . . but that's because I know the people that you're talking about. I just don't see why other people would think it's funny.
-- my dad

This text is not exactly what I would call an AMAZING accomplishment, and it is barely passable as LITERATURE.
-- anonymous review

If you do nothing else this summer, you may be the type of person who could read this book . . . maybe.
-- Pat Carey

Growing Up Irish Catholic, and Surviving My Mom's Eleven Sisters

By
Pat Carey

ᴘ
Aventine Press LLC

A note on names within the book: I have tried my best not to change the names and faces in the following pages . . . many of the people I grew up with have sufficiently funny names, and very few of them are innocent.

Published by Aventine Press, LLC
2208 Cabo Bahia
Chula Vista, CA 91914, USA

www.aventinepress.com

ISBN: 1-59330-123-5
Printed in the United States of America

For my dad, my mom and the family that created this book;
also thanks to my girlfriend Diane, my writing buddies JP
and Kevin, and the incomparable Gajohnson

Stories

The ANDOVER To

Andover's Own Newspaper Since

VOLUME 79 NUMBER 26

ANDOVER, MASSACHUSETTS, AP

One Family Easter Parade

EASTER DRESS REHEARSAL – Jean Chalifour and his family, ready for an Easter parade. Left to right, Laurie, Mary Elayne, Sandra, Jane, Edith, Mr. and Mrs. Chalifour, Dianne, Cheryl, Nancee, Brenda and Ann. Front row, Kathi and Renee. (Cole)

Father Boasts 12 Daughters

(A Townsman News Feature)

If you are going to go so far as to have twelve children, you might as well make it an even dozen females!

This is the way Jean J. Chalifour looks at it, and he ought to know. His house is filled with the chatter of big girls, little girls and medium sized girls who are both daughters and sons to the 41-year-old An-

One by one, the daughters are: Cheryl, 18, a dance student at the Boston Conservatory of Music; Edith, 16; Dianne, 15, a member of the Andover High School championship girls' gym team; Jane, 12; Sandra, 11; Nancee, 10; Mary Elayne, 9; Brenda, 7; Laurie, 6; Ann, 5; Kathi, 4 and Renee, 3.

Home Sweet Home

The Chalifours live on an 11-acre estate (286 S. Main St.) which

and forth in a station-wagon bus

The Chalifour children ar children like other children ar consequently not always jubilar at the prospect of tackling the car of the expansive lawn and othe home upkeep projects. They kee most of the grumbling undercove however, because their father in sists upon and gets cooperatio His wife says he is "positive the head of the household",

Potatoes

Thinking about my Irish Catholic background always invokes two images: potatoes strewn about the house and a burning bush. Some people can point to a day or a moment that encapsulates their ethnic experience and sense of identity. For me, one day when I was ten years old is forever etched in my mind as my Irish experience. Up until that day, I had only a vague sense of Irish culture. Our favorite Irish dish was boiled dinner, basically a huge pot filled with pork shoulder, cabbage, carrots, turnip, and of course potatoes. Outsiders laugh at the concept of Irish cuisine, claiming that meat and vegetables put into hot water does not constitute a recipe. Or that the term boiled dinner is no different than baked food or fried stuff. My parents once served boiled dinner vegetables to my vegetarian girlfriend, who complained that all the vegetables tasted liked salty, soaked pork. Obviously, she missed the whole point of boiled dinner. The closest to an Irish cooking recipe that I have seen among other cultures was a dish on the menu in a Vietnamese restaurant – it was called ten things in a pot.

So this formidable day began like any other, a gaggle of my mom's sisters storming up to the house with a big idea. My mom is one of twelve girls, the Chalifour girls. Her dad, my

Grampy, had given up after twelve attempts to make a boy. People often explained the sheer size of my mom's family with the comment *like a good Catholic family*. One of my uncle's would tell somebody, "Oh yeah, he pumped out twelve girls, like a good Catholic family." And often the expression was punctuated with a throbbing fist to show the pumping that had been referred to. I wasn't sure exactly what it meant to be a good Catholic family, but it seemed to have something to do with girls, and sex. Grampy had bought himself a vanity plate that read GIRLS, and cruised around in his car like the town pimp.

I heard a ruckus on the patio, and found a few of my mom's sisters haggling over a plan for the day. I looked through my swarming aunts to see our neighbor Mr. Walsh, frozen mid-stride in front of his house. I think Mr. Walsh was in his mid-nineties when we moved in, which would put him trickling over the hundred barrier on this particular day. Unimpressed by the noise and excitement of my aunts, Mr. Walsh stood frigid a mere forty feet or so from our patio, poised and posed in front of his house and staring down the growing bush that was overtaking it. He stared deep into the green menace, somehow watching it grow, zoning in on fleshy roots that were even now slowly crawling up the shingles of his house. Or maybe he had just happened to freeze this time facing the house and the bush. His mind may have been elsewhere as he gathered the strength for his next movement, maybe an eye twitch or a slight shift of his foot.

We often saw Mr. Walsh in these frozen stages, cryogenics of living cells moving slowly across the lawn. He moved slowly for a person, for sure. But as a changing lawn ornament he was pretty fast, downright sprightly. We would go downtown for a couple of hours and come back to find him in a slightly different arrangement. Friends came over that actually thought he was a statue, they would come and go without seeing any movement or progress. Somehow when we turned our backs he would eventually be on the other side of the lawn, or posed on the steps of his house. He was challenging us to a drawn out game of red light, green light, and he was damn good at it. We hardly ever saw his movements, and wondered if this might be an elaborate publicity stunt for the wax museum. What strength he could gather seemed entirely directed against the amorphous bush that threatened his house. Often his crooked poses were accessorized with weaponry, like a G.I.Joe. He would face the bush with one arm raised holding clippers, hedge trimmers, his beebee gun, all pointed against the tyranny of the leafy menace before him. But this morning was a quiet day for Mr. Walsh, frozen by the bush. Perhaps an onlooker might have thought he was mesmerized by its growing vines, stopped to ponder the Emersonian beauty of the natural world. But after the days events had unfolded we would look back to see the cold stare of a man pushed too far, the quiet solitude of plotting before an attack.

Just a stone's throw away my aunts were plotting their own schemes. It's difficult to know the severity of their plans until they come to fruition, as even planning hors d'oeuvres becomes a sort of intricate war room strategy. And there's always an army of girls ready to carry it out. This particular brainstorm involved a blurb in the paper about an overstocked farm in western Massachusetts. A sudden and prolonged rainstorm the night before had left much of their root vegetables uncovered, and many of them would rot if not brought in. It seemed they had potatoes that would go unharvested due to a lack of farmhands. My aunts were seasoned gardeners growing up, and they certainly had no similar shortage of farm hands. They began to dream of western Massachusetts, of fields and fields of potatoes. A plan solidified by the core Chalifour sisters is not easily torn asunder. Encircled in a football huddle they stared down at the four lines of newspaper text laid out on the patio, and began to make lists of vans and trucks that they could commandeer.

Late in the evening the girl's army returned in a caravan of dodge caravans, and minivans and trucks. They created a virtual blockade on our small road, as other cars could scarcely maneuver around the pile up of potato transporting vehicles. My brother Ray and I were enlisted to carry loads of potatoes around the back of the house to the patio. The potatoes were soft and slimy, and covered in thick mud. There were mounds of mud in the trunks of cars, overflowing out of glove compartments, and spilling out into the street. Bundles of mud were then dropped onto the patio, where other soldiers were ready to sift through the wreckage for survivors and set them in rows. One of my aunts had taken the hose from the front of the house, sliced the end open, and used duct tape to fasten it to the kitchen faucet. My sisters Michelle and Julie came in and looked around. Michelle laughed, "Dad is gonna love this." My two sisters were immediately put to task, hosing off the rows of potatoes which were then passed along from one aunt to another and into the house.

From the patio we saw Mr. Walsh back at the bush, this time his hand was drawn back with a large pair of cloth-cutting shears. We figured the bush was due for a violent alteration when his hand finally came back down. That gave the bush anywhere from twenty-five to forty-five minutes to plan it's defense and retaliation. Ray and I continued to pile hundreds of potatoes onto the patio, and Michelle and Julie kept at their washing station. We were never privy to the full Chalifour girls' strategic plans, told only the details of our specific role and ignorant of the real designs of the empire we served. We had no knowledge of where these hundreds of potatoes were headed in our small house, and who would be responsible for this chaos when my dad got home.

I dropped a load of mud onto the patio, then searching with my fingers noticed that this pile had no potatoes in it. I stopped for a minute and sculpted a little figure with my hands.

"What's that?" Michelle asked.

"It's Mr. Walsh." I kneaded another stack of mud into a high wave that hung over the figures head. "And this is the green bush, overtaking him." I piled the mud on top of my Mr. Walsh, then glanced up to see the other statue of him. "That's a big friggan pair of scissors," I said. "That bush is in for an ass whoopin'."

"Hey," Michelle called me over to whisper, "I think a lot of these potatoes are rotten." This didn't come as a big surprise, as my mom's sisters had a habit of bringing rotten food to our house. Their leftovers became like hand-me-downs when they got too old for them to eat. Someone would march up the street from my grandmother's house with a generous offering of food that had almost gone bad. My dad was always subtly and otherwise trying to let them know that if the food was too old for them to eat, we didn't want it. But whenever someone was about to throw out food down the street, one of the Chalifour girls would always perk up, "No wait, bring it to the Carey's house. They don't care, they'll eat anything." Well, they were half right. Half of the time my dad would get his hands on it and we would throw it out, and the other half my mom would hide it deep in a casserole.

Michelle picked up a soft potato and easily put her thumb deep inside it. "Why are we keeping these?" She made a face, but defiance was as risky as independent thought under the Chalifour regime. She shook her thumb and the potato rolled onto the pile headed inside.

I echoed her sentiments, "Dad is gonna love this." The bomb was set on a two hour timer, when my dad would return home, and we hoped that following rank would be defense enough to keep us out of it.

After our work was complete we were allowed to leave our stations. Ray and I met up with my sisters at the hosing off area. We hosed ourselves off like so many piles of potato filled mud, then crept inside to see the damage. Only in the calm of the aftermath, did we begin to realize the full consequences of our involvement in this Chalifour charade. Now to understand the current state of the house and its subsequent effect on my dad, it's important to have some history of our house. For about the first ten years of my life we had lived in that house. The first year and a half was spent without any of the interior work finished. The outside of the house was in good shape, but inside was a mere skeleton of a family home. We designed separate rooms with furniture, claiming territory between bureaus and chairs. For us, it was like living in a fort you built from scrap wood. For my dad, he worked hard to slowly improve the house. A year before the potatoes arrived, we had put in windows that locked without the use of ten inch nails. And we no longer woke in the middle of the night to screams of *Rain, rain, someone get the towels.* With the windows came three skylights that brightened up the house. And finally, just two months before the potato incident, our house had been outfitted with wall to wall carpets. It still gave us a strange feeling to take our shoes off as we came into the house. For the previous nine and a half years, the rule was that you had to wear shoes in the house, shoes or slippers at all times. We had wooden floors -- not hardwood floors as people call them, but unfinished floors which were quick to give little naked feet splinters as they passed between the few braided area rugs.

We took our shoes off and wandered through the house, assessing the damage first with a playful curiosity and then through the eyes of my dad. "Dad is gonna kill somebody," Ray muttered.

Michelle was the oldest and settled his fears, "Just stick together and hopefully it'll be one of mom's sisters."

Newspaper had been haphazardly thrown first across the kitchen counters, then the floor, and onto the dining room table. When the newspaper ran out, pieces of paper towel, napkins, and scraps of tissue were laid out across the living room, on the edge of the stairs, and throughout the bedrooms. An old sheet covered my parents bed, which in turn was covered with rows and piles of potatoes. My sisters had cleaned much of the mud off, but these potatoes were still leaking mud and soft potato innards all over the house. Many areas had stacks of paper and potatoes rising a foot off the ground, like a giant potato and paper lasagna, with a muddy cheese substitute.

The aunts were bickering loudly downstairs. We figured they were panicking, figuring a way to evade my dad for a few months. One of them rushed to the phone. The excitement it turns out was over dinner options, and my aunt was on the phone calling for a pizza. Later someone suggested trying to clean up, which was quickly shot down by three other sisters, each with her own reason. One claimed the potatoes needed more drying time, a second declared that the situation was far beyond clean up, and the third yelled out that the pizza had arrived, which pretty much ended all discussion.

We all stood around the living room, as the seats and couches were fully covered with rotting potatoes. We were on our feet eating pizza and watching a movie when a car rumbled into the driveway. The emergency brake made a loud rip and the car door banged shut. My dad had spent years trying to improve his house and keep the Chalifour girls from delivering rotten food to it. My little sister sensed the tension and put a finger to her mouth, "Uh oh."

My dad opened the door, kicking a potato across the room before he looked down to see what it was. His eyes scanned the floor of potatoes and rose to meet the crew of aunts standing with their pizza. He looked as if he was talking but no sound came out. Then he took a breath, "The rug."

My aunt took a bite of pizza and mumbled, "Yeah, we were worried it would rain, get 'em even more wet."

My dad picked up a potato and looked at it like it was a new and strange vegetable. "The new rug, the skylights."

My aunt opened a mouth full of sausage pizza to squeeze out, "Yeah, that's great. We figured the skylights would be good for drying out the potatoes."

My dad drew back his arm and stared down her sausage cheese throat, taking aim with a soft, rotting potato. "Eeeaahhhchk." A strange low scream echoed through the room. I looked to my aunt and then my dad, but the noise came from outside the house. My dad ran outside to find Mr. Walsh frozen in battle with the green menace, a red tank of gasoline by his side, and flames dancing around his slow moving frame. The bush was engulfed in fire, which spread to the edge of the grass and the edge of Mr. Walsh's pants and jacket. My dad grabbed the hose as I rushed to turn the sink on, my aunt's strange contraption still leading out of the kitchen and onto the patio. My dad doused the fiery bush and the feisty Mr. Walsh for several minutes. All wet, Mr. Walsh seemed shrunk to about half his normal statue but was lucky to have survived without major burns. The bush too, was lucky enough to survive the attack, and grew even more fierce the following year.

My aunt wandered outside just as the commotion was dying down. "See, if we had left em outside they would've got all wet."

My dad turned with a big smile, then doused her twice as thoroughly as he had Mr. Walsh.

I always connected that memory with my concept of being Irish, a moment of family strife and potatoes. I guess we were a good Irish Catholic family, but somehow my image of Ireland lies somewhere between a burning Mr. Walsh and a house covered with muddy, rotting potatoes. And well, how the neighborhood comes together in times of crisis.

The annual Headmaster's banquet . . . A joyous occasion . . . When all hearts were happy because of the approaching holidays . . .

St. John's

Growing up Catholic, we went to quite a few ceremonies. It seemed that every other weekend we had some kind of reception at the church, well usually at the church. When I was little the family used to have ceremonies at my house. I vaguely remember my first communion: I was five, and a priest showed up at the door. He laid some cloths on the table, whipped out a briefcase full of booze, red church wine, and at his signal my mom put on the Carpenters record. "Everything is coming over me . . ." Karen Carpenter backed up the priest as he did that science guy thing where he pours wine and water back and forth between glasses. And then the Carpenters big chorus, "I'm on the top of the world, lookin', down on creation and the only explanation I can find, is the love that I found ever since you've been around, you're love put me at the top of the world." Then the priest put his hands on my shoulders and started muttering. It was like a scene from the Exorcist or a documentary about cults.

My mom is the third oldest, so as kids we took part in a lot of my aunts' wedding ceremonies. I had been a ring bearer and usher many times, but never an altar boy. Until one of my aunts decided that she wanted her entire ceremony to be staffed with family. My brother Ray and I were chosen as the altar boys. The fact that we were never trained or ordained, or had never paid much attention in church was irrelevant. We were picked despite protests, like the bright green bridesmaid dresses. My father, who had himself spent a couple years as an altar boy, was one of the loudest in his disapproval, but clearly had no power over his sister-in-law's use of his children.

The groom was an old high school buddy of my dad's, Bernie Mulholland. So the day before the wedding my dad dug up his high school yearbook and told stories of his old days at St. John's. It was an all boys Catholic school, and a boarding school at the time my dad went there. He showed us some pictures of the Xaverian Brothers that ran the school, with nicknames like Brother Blockhead and The Duck. My favorite nicknames were Brother Bourbon Moonshine, after the swaggering, muttering Robin Moonsane, and Brother Holiday, a ninety-something year old brother who would fall asleep in class, and was named for the holiday the students would get when he died. We were given a tour of my dad's old buddies, like David Hoar, who had spent countless hours listening to kids tell him, "Look, your mother's a Hoar, your sister's a Hoar." And of course Bernie Mulholland, supposedly famous for giving the finger in all his yearbook pictures. He had slid into many photos for clubs and activities he didn't belong in, and always found some way to secretly flip off the camera, or so the story goes. We were shown pictures of Bernie waving, scratching his nose, and touching his knee, all with the claim that these were undercover *fuck yous* to the administration. I looked forward to seeing this Bernie and showing him a nice, long unmistakable middle finger to see if he was still that edgy character of the St. John's legend.

My brother and I went to St. John's high school, but years after they had done away with all the dormitories. My dad continued his tour. "Oh yeah, another flip em the bird from old Mulholland. Ole' Bernie always gets it in there somehow."

Me and my brother Ray looked on but were unconvinced. He looked a friendly, almost kiss-ass student with all of his waving and pointing, pictures ripe for a St. John's brochure.

"Hey, here's a picture of the old two finger flip." My dad leaned back with a knowing laugh.

I leaned forward with a what are you talking about, "What?"

"C'mon, the two finger flip. Hit em in the business in the hallway." He was convinced my brother and I had experienced this at least at St. John's.

Ray assured my dad that we had no knowledge of this hitting them in the business he spoke of. "Uh, dad, we didn't really whack each other in the nads a whole lot at school."

"Are you kidding? You always had to put up your protection going down the hallway." He showed us the proper method for making a hand cup to protect yourself, and I guess to keep your business up and running. "Never know at St. John's when someone's gonna snap you one."

I leaned over and snapped a finger at Ray's pants. "St. John's."

"Get off. St. John's yourself." He whacked back, but I had my shield ready as my dad had showed us.

My dad looked on with disapproval. "Well, good shield, but you don't say St. John's when you do it, we were all at St. John's."

The priest who did all the family ceremonies was a big guy I like to call Father Rodney. He'd get up on the altar, rumble and ramble, and suddenly lost amidst some strange metaphor, would stick two fingers in his collar and give it the old no respect Rodney Dangerfield tug. This would provide a transition into some odd story of growing up near my grandfather or a time he saw one of my cousin's crying and left her to cry. Father Rodney would lead up to some unattainable point, pull at his collar and move on. His other transition was a deep "heh," almost a cough, but it's intonation carried a thought provoking sort of "heh." The trouble is he would use it only when he said something that required no real deeper examination, like "Cousin Ellen is a girl, heh." We would all wait while he paused and looked around so we could consider this fact.

My brother and I were told to be at the church an hour and a half early so that Father Rodney could tell us what to do during the ceremony. While we were waiting for him to show, Ray and I were hanging out in the back with Tommy. He's our six year old cousin, the ring bearer in the wedding. I told Tommy to tell Ray St. John's and then hit him in the business. Then I told him where the business was and he almost caught Ray, but Ray got his protection up quick. Of course this entertained us for an hour or so. Little Tommy knew everything he was supposed to do during the mass, but we still had only a vague idea about maybe bringing the wine from somewhere when Rodney looked thirsty.

The scheduled crash course had to be condensed when Father Rodney showed up just minutes before the ceremony. He handed us two white pull over outfits, like hospital gowns with gold ribbons sewn on. "Put these on, heh." We followed him to the edge of the altar and he turned to give us the instructions: "Follow my lead." Then he pointed to two chairs on the altar and we sat down, in full view of everyone and too far from each other to whisper, "What the hell do we do now?" Father Rodney left us slumped in baggy white sheets, waiting and wondering what we would do when he turned to us.

The wedding was going along smoothly, and we hadn't been winked at or mumbled to so I figured we were doing fine. Well fine except that Ray had fallen asleep, and some of our relatives were pointing and laughing. The middle-finger guy and my aunt came up on the altar, and our little friend Tommy brought the rings down the aisle and stood by their side. Father Rodney turned around to face us, after grumbling something to the crowd. He looked at Ray slowly melting out of his chair, then back to me. He nodded, "Heh." I shrugged my shoulders slightly and tried to give off a calm, but inquisitive look of, "What the hell am I supposed to do?" Father Rodney responded with a series of slightly different hehs, a language of his own creation. He became stuck on the "heh," repeating it in strange tones like a warped record. It was a deep, guttural "heh," and one of my aunts yelled out, "I think he's choking." Ray woke up, startled, and wiped a bit of drool from his white outfit.

My dad left the first row and approached the altar, perhaps with his altar boy experience to guide us into the next step of the ceremony. He walked up to me with a severe look that told me to follow him just off the altar, where he gave me a glass bottle that I brought to Father Rodney. Rodney thanked me with a soft, soothing "Heh." As my dad approached the bride and groom to vacate the altar, Bernie smiled and gave a soft wave. I stared at a long middle finger that seemed extended slightly above the rest. My dad smiled and made a little fist in solidarity, whispering, " St. John's." Little Tommy yelled St. John's, then reeled back his right arm and gave my dad a solid shot straight through his balls, before he even had the chance to make a protection. My dad fell to one knee and Father Rodney turned to the people and then to my dad. He looked confused and shouted, "Heh."

My dad gathered his strength and with a hoarse voice whispered to Tommy, "You don't say St. John's."

Tough guys cry

At the age of 3, I had already established a reputation for bad behavior. I carried with it a sort of cute cockiness, like the sex appeal of mafia thugs. Put outside to play with my brother and sisters, I would look around the yard, then pace the patio and take a seat on the wooden steps. The wooden steps were used as a holding area for misbehaving kids, a time out from the general population. Sent to the prison yard for recreation, I chose solitary confinement as some kind of psychological power move. One of my aunts would come over and encourage me to go play with the other kids. "Why don't you go play? Look, Ray's playing with a football. Don't you want to play catch?"

I would raise an eyebrow and respond slowly, as if I were dumbing down my three year old philosophy for their benefit. "Listen . . . I'm gonna be bad today."

"No, you can go play, you haven't done anything wrong." They seemed more upset by this calm demeanor than my actual bad behavior. "Pat, honey why don't you go play with the kids. Look, you're sisters are starting a double dutch. Do you jumprope?"

I made a face to the effect of, no, I don't jump over ropes and then continued. "I'm gonna go play for a few minutes, and then I'll do something bad, and you'll tell me to go sit on the stairs."

My aunt seemed confused.

I spoke more slowly to clarify the situation. "Look, we both know I'm gonna be bad. So why not just sit on the stairs now and save all that trouble."

As I grew older, I developed a knack for negotiating, getting into trouble and then weaseling my way out of it. My parents used to leave the four of us kids at home, with a list of chores that had to be done. Shortly before my parents came home, my sisters would go into panic mode, finishing up the chores. Usually my brother Ray and I had already racked up a list of transgressions that added to the fact that we had done no chores. My older sister Michelle would begin to list off what she would report to mom and dad. I would gather everyone together in the living room, sometimes as my parents' car was pulling into the driveway. In a sibling huddle I would call for a truce and a pact, with a phrase that became famous among my family and friends, "Hey, how about nobody tell on no one."

"What? We didn't do anything wrong. And we did all the chores." Michelle, who would later in life become a lawyer, didn't see the justice in this.

"Yeah, we got a few things on you two. Ray and I will tell on you guys." Ray looked on confused.

"Like what? What did we do?" This was like the old question posed time and time again to the mafia: *Protection money? Protection from who?*

"Well, we'll make some shit up." After listening to a list of possible accusations my sisters would generally agree to a mutually beneficial arrangement. I would couch our deals in terms of sibling love, and our need to pull together against the tyranny of parents and adults. *Friends help each other out, make sure that nobody's bar catches on fire and that nobody slips and falls on an ice pick, capiche.*

I found a lot of success in steering tattletales down the right path and keeping my nose clean. Then I found my nemesis in a fifteen year old girl with braces -- the baby-sitter. She was a skinny, freckle-faced neighbor paid about seventy-five cents to provide muscle and a full report to my parents. She carried a flower covered briefcase and pretended to be a teacher, rewarding us with gold star stickers if we played along. But beneath that facade, Becky Dow was a ruthless confidante to the adult world and a difficult mind to bend with psychological torture. We tried to threaten to tell on her, but my parents always gave more credence to her version of the story.

One night my brother pulled out a big knife and threatened suicide -- I used the distraction to make an escape. I took off down the street in my pajamas to avoid an early bedtime. Ray was indicted on two accounts, scaring Becky with talk of suicide and touching the big knife. I was chased down the street and then tied to my bed with a jump rope. This, I figured, I could finally use against Becky, and win a little clout with the parents by playing up the cruel baby-sitter card. My parents came home and scolded us. I pleaded with them and told how Becky had chased me down the street before tying me up with a jump rope. They thanked her and gave her an extra quarter.

In the first grade, my general demeanor as a punk and a trouble maker quickly became public knowledge. I could no longer hide among the bad deeds of other kids, or rely on the frail psychological character of my kindergarten teacher. Now at school I was in trouble constantly. I used to have a scheduled fight with the same kid, Jon, at recess every day. I wore my tiny jean jacket, which became a symbol of my toughness and bad attitude. It was my signature outfit, kind of like Michael Jackson with his red and black leather jacket, except a little more tough. It's basically the same size and style that skinny fashion girls wear today. I would roll up the sleeves and meet Jon in front of the tire swing. We had a sort of camaraderie to our battles, and the class would sway its allegiances based on the outcomes of the fight. The other kids usually rooted for the person who was winning, but they were sensitive, and by the end of the day always sided with the loser of the fight. One time I showed up at school with a broken arm, and a cast sticking out of my jean jacket sleeve. The crowd's sympathy of course went to an injured fighter willing to fight, but quickly swayed when I used the cast to my advantage.

They say that every tough guy has a weakness. Like Superman's troubles with kryptonite or Ted Kennedy's weakness for girls and booze, I too had a weakness. My eyes were very sensitive, causing them to water at awkward times. Basically, office lights and repeated camera flashes would make my eyes tear up. So despite my reputation at school, at the barbershop and the dentist I had a different demeanor. I had to endure constant pity from the dental aids: "Are you sure you're OK honey? This really shouldn't be hurting you too bad?" At the barbershop Tony would taunt me while he cut my hair, "What did I stab you with the scissors? Is your mother making you get a haircut? Do I do that bad a job, you're a walking friggan advertisement for me. C'mon in, be my next happy customer. Just look at this kid with the shaved head. So he's crying a little, but he looks alright, eh?" At least these visits were only about every four months for the dentist, and even less for the barbershop. Ray and I would get haircuts about twice a year, shave our heads and then wait until the hair began to cover our eyes and shave them again. We thought it was funny when people we knew seemed to always have the same basic haircut. "That guy must live at a damn barbershop, he always has the same hairdo. What a weirdo."

I continued to get into fights at school and trouble at home, so my parents kept trying to push me into activities. There wasn't much I wanted to do until Ray won a bike at the

YMCA swimathon. He rode his little Huffy on dirt paths and made jumps out of bricks and wood planks down the middle of our street. It seemed the perfect compliment to my reckless ways and my jean jacket, a new dirt bike to power down bumpy trails and fly over homemade ramps. Ray and I were already on the swim team at the YMCA, although he was more serious about it. I was more into the rec room, playing bumper pool tournaments for pizza slices. My parents would watch practice from the window in the rec room, and often saw me pop up in the middle of a lap, look around for the coach, and then head back the other way. Ray was dedicated to swimming. I just liked hanging around downtown and chatting with the old guys in the steam room. I was always looking for shortcuts and trying to get out of practice early.

I asked my parents for a bike, and they told me we couldn't afford it. I had a little scooter I used to cruise around town on, but I was ready for something a little more flashy. I strolled by the bike shop checking out the BMX bikes and all the funky colored pads. They had the cool patterns of Trapper Keeper notebook covers. I was checking out an all chrome bike with no pads, a stunt man's ride with none of the little kid safety features. I checked with the YMCA rules, which stated that the winners of the swimathon would receive any bike of their choice from the local shop. The winners were defined as the boy and girl who raised the most money, or anyone who swam one hundred laps. I entered the swimathon, then got ten bucks from my parents as a sponsor. I didn't really have the boyscout, paper boy of the year mentality to raise the most money. I had no interest in door to door sales or trying to be cute for other people's parents. So I decided to swim one hundred laps, raise ten bucks, and win that shiny silver ride.

I threw off my jean jacket and pulled on a saggy speedo and goggles. The coaches paced the side of the pool, preventing any half lap strategy I may have concocted. After what may have been an hour of swimming, fully exhausted, I flailed my arms and legs in a kind of almost drowning side-stroke, and barely found the wall. That was about lap forty. I think that my hard work at practices had prepared me to swim about twenty laps, the rest was mere desire for that metallic huffy. I continued swimming, like a castaway heading for shore. I took in gulps of water, laid on my back and kicked for a couple laps, and then sprinted in a splashing frenzy for the ninety ninth lap. I turned for the last lap, completely depleted. As my parents and brother cheered from the side, I drifted down the pool. Barely able to kick or paddle, I floated slowly to the end of the pool, toward a new bike. After my hundredth lap, I collapsed on the tile floor, then stumbled off to the steam room to tell the old men of my triumphant swim.

Mary, who also won a bike, had swum about fifteen laps, but had raised fifteen hundred dollars. Supposedly her dad was the CEO of some company where she had gone door to door, or office to office, smiling with her sign up sheet in a t-shirt that read the boss's daughter. I had raised a record breaking low ten dollars for the YMCA. We were called together to take a picture for the local newspaper. They showed up with my chrome beauty, an adult bike that had to be special ordered to fit my dimensions. I had talked my way out of the kiddy bikes, quoting their policy of pick any bike in the shop. Mary stood by her pink kid's bike with a dress covered in different kinds of birds. She looked as if she were being attacked by the birds as a smile crept onto her face. I stood proud, with my jean jacket rolled up to the elbows, leaning against my new wheels. The photographer flashed a heavy light and snapped repeated pictures. She kept pleading with me to smile, to show my teeth, to say things like cheese and YMCA and swimming. As Mary yelled out these words on command, I stared down the camera with a slight smirk of check out my bike. It made Mary's bike look like a tricycle. As we said around Boston those days, it was wicked pissah.

After about five bulb flashes my eyes began to water and tear. I held a tough face as tears filled my cheeks. My eyes glossy and wet, the camera lady asked me if I was scared. I laughed, and she snapped another picture. And that would be the shot that printed in the paper -- Mary with a big teethy smile in her bird attack dress, and me with my open mouth almost smiling, my jean jacket matching the tough chrome bike, and my face covered in tears.

Baseball

My older brother and sister would test out activities for the family, the way science tortures animals for the benefit of humans. Ray and Michelle would get signed up for all sorts of strange activities, and the ones that stuck would filter down to me and my little sister Julie. Michelle spent a few weeks in girl scouts meeting the snobby neighborhood girls, who were not quite as catty as their moms.

Ray actually enjoyed the boy scouts at first, until my dad became involved. They were not the most successful father and son team on many of the projects, the worst being their legendary performance at the soap box derby. Many of the other fathers were engineers, auto specialists, or general craftsman. My dad's high school teaching experience in no way prepared him to build a small wooden car that would race down a ramp. My brother's car didn't have the sleek design and alternate building materials of the other contestants. His car was a block of wood with wheels, with a small angle dug out of the front as if with a spoon. The cars were timed going down a long ramp and jumping the small hill at the bottom. A few cars were not fast enough to make the last hill, and had to be weighted down to increase their speed. A can of change was available for extra weight, and the contestant was penalized for each penny taped onto the car. A few cars required two cents or four cents to make the last bit of ramp. Ray and my dad, with their patented, sleek block of wood design, barely made it down the ramp on the first go, with no chance of racing over the last incline. First one penny at a time, and later by the handful, change was added to the block and the car was re-tested. The wood soon became a mere lower layer to a car design dominated by pennies and duct tape. Hours later Ray arrived home defeated: "Some people needed a couple cents for their car to make the ramp, at the worst four or five. I set a soap box derby record with a buck seventeen taped to my car." Ray quit the next day, and Julie and I never became scouts.

These were not isolated trial and error activities. Michelle and Ray were forced into taking Latin at school, which put them among some of the more strange teachers and students at the middle school. Instead of field trips to Mexican restaurants like the Spanish class, the Latin students were forced to wear sheets to school and participate in an event called Saturnalia, a bizarre auction selling off students as personal attendants. Julie and I later enrolled in Spanish classes. The only trial that remains a mystery is pre-school. Michelle, the oldest, was sent off to pre-school at age four. After that, for none of us attended pre-school, having to wait for kindergarten to run under parachutes and eat playdough.

The activities that stuck we would all do together, like swim lessons and summer park and rec. These were mostly successful, excluding a brief stint as a family tap dance troupe. Julie and Michelle stayed with ballet dancing and gymnastics, and Ray and I ended up on sports teams together. We got involved in town sports leagues for soccer, swimming, and baseball.

Once in a while my parents efforts blossomed, and we would find ourselves frozen in a perfect moment, like the 1982 baseball championship. Ray and I played together that year on the Saints, just two steps up from the T-ball league where infants hack at a ball on the end of a pole like a baseball piñata party. Town baseball had about seven leagues, which put us in the farm league for the farm league for the farm league for the high school team. Not too bad for a couple of home town kids with big dreams and no real talent for the game.

Our coach, Robert Sides, was Bobby Junior's dad. Bobby Junior, one of the worst players among a pool of low talent, was somehow a pitcher. They called him Bobby Junior even though coach Robert never went by Bobby. Robert always wore his college uniform to our games, a throwback to the days "when baseball was fun," and apparently when his body fit into that uniform. A low hanging gut peeked out below an angry peacock and the number 11. "The only thing better than being number one, is being it twice." He would look at us and laugh, a giggling pre-teen in his sporty half-shirt.

Today, coach had a severe look in his eyes, the sort of Mr. Sides mentality that had probably matured his name from Bobby to Robert. He looked across the field, and twice tucked in his shirt which bounced defiantly back above his belly button. "Alright soldiers, gather round." We knelt around him. I stared up past his belly, but caught a glimpse up his shirt and turned away. "Let's focus up here. After careful consideration, we're starting Bobby Junior on the mound."

We let out a collective moan and one of us yelled, "Yeah, thanks dad."

"Often the difference between a lousy team and a good team, is good coaching. The difference between a good coach and a great coach, is good coaching. And the line between an OK coach and a great coach is as fine as the third base line."

I looked at Ray then stared back into his belly, looking for some explanation.

"OK, it's real important to obey the signs today. Whatever sign I give, you need to respond and just go. Like the four horse with a little jockey screaming go, go baby."

Bobby Junior spoke up, "Like a horse?" He looked more like a jockey.

"You're pitching today, Junior."

"Yeah, daddy."

"One more time, here's the most important sign. When I do this" -- he rubbed his bearded chin with a hand, that thumb on one side pensive stroke of genius. "This is the sign for stealing a base. When I give the sign, just go."

Bobby perked up, "Like the four horse, daddy?

"Don't think about it, just go, go. Don't think just go."

My mom had a habit of confusing us with the conflicting commands of *don't think, just do* and *think before you act.* I popped Ray an elbow and leaned over, "Think before you act."

Ray laughed and stroked his beardless chin. "Don't think, just do."

Coach Robert finished his speech, or forgot the rest of it, and we wandered onto the field. I stumbled off to deep left field, left out as we called it. Outfield in this league was a place to stick folks who couldn't catch the ball. Ray had found his way to third base when our sure gloved Ralphy caught the chicken pox. He turned down the offer of Ralphy's glove though it was a nicer one, worried about the pox that might be nestling in the fingers. My parents and eight or nine aunts cheered us along through the innings, giving the concession box a rare boost in business and screwing up next season's inventory.

In the bottom of the eighth inning, I stepped up to bat with one out away, down 3 runs to 1. Coach Robert shoved a helmet on my head and tapped it down over my eyes. "Don't worry about getting a hit, just get on base."

"No problem coach." This might seem a strange dilemma, but I was as well known for getting on base as I was for not getting hits. I approached the plate, tipped the helmet up so I could see, and dug my toes deep into the dirt. As the pitcher looked for a sign I crouched down near the plate, and then lower, hovering with my chest about a foot off the ground. The pitcher hurled a fast ball that bounced in the dirt and into the catcher's shin.

I had the most walks of any player in the league, perfecting my low crouch technique throughout the season. Pitchers would consistently roll balls across the plate at my ankles, or hit me with a wild pitch out of frustration. Either way, I would make it to first base. Apparently, the pitcher can earn called strikes by throwing the ball where my legitimate strike zone should be, up near my head. But two steps up from t-ball, my no swing batting technique had helped us into the finals.

Three balls, two strikes now in the eighth inning, full count. A zinger headed straight for my head. I ducked just in time, which is more than I can say for the catcher. The umpire called a strike, but I took off to first base as the catcher stood up dazed, finding the ball a minute later.

Ray came up to bat, the tying run at the plate. Now Ray was too tall and maybe too proud to use my crouch technique, but was a pretty poor hitter in his own right. He considered any contact between the ball and bat to be a hit, claiming victory anytime he made an out without completely missing three balls in a row. Ray was actually a good athlete, an impressive swimmer and not a bad soccer player. But for some reason, he had never really come around as a batter. He was one of the few people I ever saw strike out in t-ball.

Ray stood holding the bat at his chest like a bouquet of flowers, offering his out to the pitcher. The first pitch came right where the bat had been, but Ray chopped at it low, like it was rolling across the plate at one of my crouches. Then came a low ball and he snapped the bat across his chest, as if on some kind of one pitch delay. A mere foot away from the ball, Ray had at least swung hard, and the momentum carried him a step toward the mound. He backed away and stepped out of the batter's box, searching the stands.

The crowd began to gather behind Ray's impossible dream. My aunts led our fans into a chant of Mondo, Mondo. This was a family nickname coming from Raymond, the full version of the nickname being Raymondo. Mondo was Ray's nickname from the swim team, where he had a reputation as an up and coming talent. He stepped up to the plate, tapped his bat in the dirt, and stood a little taller, the anti-crouch stance. The chants of Mondo grew louder, perhaps my aunts had begun to bully the other team's fans into shouting as well. The chant was just loud and strange enough to cause the other team to begin fidgeting in the field, wondering if perhaps Ray was about to turn into Mondo, busting green Hulk muscles through his Saints shirt. The pitcher kicked a wild leg out and snapped a fast ball. Ray stepped into the pitch and drilled it out past the infield, bouncing hard toward middle field. It rolled by a surprised outfielder, who rarely had balls hit out his way. He ran to the ball and threw it about thirty feet, not reaching the infield. By the time the second baseman tracked it down, I had brought us to within one run, and Ray was halfway to third base. He reached the bag just before the throw and was safe at third, his first ever triple, having never hit the elusive double and rarely finding first base all season.

Robert stopped Bobby Junior as he was headed out to the plate, inserting a power hitter into the sorry tail end of our batting order. Our pinch hitter was the older cousin of our injured third baseman, supposedly just within the age limit of the league. He had a thin shadow of a mustache which drew complaints from the most vocal fans and their husbands. He looked off two balls, then swung hard at a slow ball and popped it up high. The catcher threw off his mask and waved the pitcher off as he headed toward the mound to get under it. Coach Robert looked on, scratching at his head as the ball came hurdling down at the catcher, a few feet away from home plate. The catcher leaned out and made a clean grab. Robert replaced his cap, looked over his players, and then stared pensively toward the field. He reached a hand to his chin, placed a thumb on one side and thoughtfully stroked his beard. Without hesitation, Ray jumped into a full stride and headed toward home plate. The crowd screamed and the catcher turned and walked to the plate. As Ray dug in for the last half of his sprint the catcher crouched down and pointed the ball in his direction. About five seconds later Ray dove head first into the catcher, who fell to the ground without losing the ball. Out! the umpire screamed. In the ninth inning we got one player to first base and never really threatened again.

After the game my dad came to console Ray, calling him very coachable where others had called him idiotic. My dad tried to place my crouching and Ray's playoff blunder in a sort of family history of sports follies. "If it makes you feel any better," he said, "in high school basketball I once scored a basket for the wrong team. And for my skill at making hook shots, I was once referred to in the paper as the hooker Ray Carey."

Dean's

We grew up amidst vague stories about my mother's professional dancing career. We heard tales of my mother taking the bus to New York for weekend gigs at age fourteen. The only legitimate source was a thin cardboard box of photos buried among the old family albums. The pictures, like the stories, were mildly scandalous shadows of my mother's former career. The photos were large black and whites, some of my mother in her professional dance duo David and Dianne. They were frozen in spins and dips, his long bushy sideburns just catching the edge of a black turtleneck. The rest were solo portraits of my mom in a white leotard and fishnet stockings, jumping into splits or making a head stand on a small card table. As kids, we marveled at her ability to stand on her head without crushing a well-formed beehive hairdo.

When we were little my mom signed all four of us up for tap dance classes. My sisters were excited to start, and my brother Ray and I were never really consulted. "It's good for people to be able to dance," she said, and then took us shopping for tap shoes. They were held at a dance studio inside of a large pink house where our teacher Miss Helen lived. Though it was called Dean's School of Dance, I still have no idea who Dean was, but we figured Miss Helen probably ate him or turned him into a coffee table. Miss Helen was a shrunken dance guru, who tapped out routines with her cane. We thought she might've been twice as tall and a professional dancer about seventy years before we met her.

Ray and I were signed into the boys' class, which consisted of Ray, Danny, and me. Danny was an awkward redhead with a big smile and not much personality. We thought he was weird and never really took to him, mostly because he seemed to enjoy being at dance class. While Danny concentrated on the lessons and yoda-like garbled speech of Miss Helen, Ray and I spent most of our time making faces at her when her back was turned. And seeing that the dance studio was covered entirely in mirrors, we were always in trouble. After kicking us out of class a few times, Miss Helen began to realize that we were not being punished, and grew worried about our lack of preparation for the upcoming dance recital. She took to withholding the after class cookies, which were thin and tasted like dog biscuits. Eventually, she found a little success by whacking at our heels with her cane. Like a an old western gunslinger she tapped at our feet and demanded we dance.

For many months Ray and I hid our tap shoes in school lockers, looking over our shoulders as we took them in and out of our backpacks. After school we were driven to the next town over, just for the chance to get tortured repeatedly by a wrinkled woman in baggy pink tights and leg warmers. It's nice to think that after all the hours we endured of dance class, Miss Helen grew accustomed to us and even began to adore our antics and foolishness. But it's not real likely. Not even a little likely. At least Miss Helen still had Danny. Clumsy and quiet, he always tried hard and kept focused, which made everyone happy. Having Danny around probably made Miss Helen a little less bothered by us. And having Danny around made us feel a little better about having to take tap dance lessons. At least we weren't Danny. We were still causing trouble and had maintained our resistance throughout.

Soon all the long hours would come to fruition. The recital. The term recital comes from ancient Greece, and it roughly means a performance piece which is almost as painful to put on as it is to watch. The dancing is important, but really a good recital is like a good drag show, cover it up with pounds of make-up and glitz and glamour, and you almost forget what you're looking at. The boys wore a stunning ensemble of white pants, gold vests covered in sequins, and styrofoam hats with red, white and blue ribbon. And during the last few weeks of class we had incorporated canes, really Ray and my favorite part of the whole thing. We could sword fight in between steps, and protect ourselves somewhat against the discipline of Miss Helen's cane. Unfortunately, though she was old and feeble, she maneuvered that thing with deft skill, just one more of her yoda-like qualities.

Our number came and went. The audience alternated with applause and laughter, and I felt we had entertained them justly. While Danny was showcasing our routine, Ray spent most of the time looking around the stage for tiny crosses of tape we were supposed to be standing on. I spent much of the time trying to keep my loose pants from sliding down, knowing that one of my aunts would be ready with a cry of "That was worth the price of admission," or "What's the rating on this show?"

My little sister waddled in for one of those little duckling pieces, a swarm of little girls bumping into each other in round, furry tutus like newborn baby chicks before their eyes open. Oohs and ahs, lots of camera flashes. A couple of them fell down, but you almost couldn't tell the way they were bunched together. Yeah, that one went a little long --the music played two minutes after it was supposed to be shut off, Mrs. Helen whispering off-stage for them to just keep tip-toeing.

And then a standing ovation as they left the stage, wild clapping and sighs of relief.

But the real focus of the recital had to be my older sister's number. Not to put down the boys tap dancing, for our highlight came with the couple of break dancing moves that filtered into our act. Maybe these days young boys incorporate rap and bitch slap each other during tap routines – we would've liked that. And our little sister's waddling chick was, well, you could almost see the birth mucus glistening off her yellow tufts of baby chick. I think they were actually supposed to be sunflowers blooming; either way, the piece was dark and realistic.

Michelle's performance really stole the show, a solo piece that came toward the end. She, and more to the point my mom, took this as a big opportunity for gaining power and prestige among the Dean's School of Dance contingent. They saw it as an informal tryout for admission into the exclusive group of older girls know as the Deanettes. If there had been a Dean around, perhaps this name would have evoked images of high school harem girls dressed in pink tights serving cocktails to a man in a white robe. In his absence, the Deanettes had a reputation as a loyal army of leaping, spinning soldiers, backing up Miss Helen's threats with tall, mean scowls traced in thick mascara. The Deanettes were an assortment of talented high school and local college girls, well very talented compared to us but lacking the ability to showcase it elsewhere. Watching them show off their skill at a little kids recital was like seeing a thirty year old boy scout achieve his badge for tying knots.

My mom was convinced that my older sister Michelle had a chance to join their ranks at an early age. Michelle was a talented dancer and gymnast, but so far lacked the snobbery and blind ambition that characterized the crew. My mom couldn't help but have visions of herself in Michelle's dancing. If only the Deanettes would have her, maybe they could begin to send her off on buses to New York. Perhaps then Michelle could begin to spin and dip with skinny beatnik poets, and someday, maybe, learn to stand upside down on a small table, elaborate hairdo completely intact. The Deanettes routines were known for wild, convulsing movements and their risqué themes. In this recital alone we had already seen them hop and skip as shoe shine boys, and waited eagerly for the final number where they would partner dance in half-man, half-woman costumes.

My mother had made some last minute changes to Michelle's routine, adding gymnastic tumbles and fine tuning her outfit. I'm not sure what look they were going for, but my mom took to Michelle's face with a vat of make-up and a butter knife like she was covering a bagel with cream cheese. Then she traced a deep, raccoon mask around her confused little eyes. The make-up didn't highlight her face, it almost doubled the size of it. Stage make-up makes your face stand out for the audience members that are far away. The back row of the recital, peering on stage from about twenty-five feet away, must've wondered about the little girl that was tumbling around a giant head, speculating that perhaps the tumbling was a result of that giant head, which threw off her balance.

Michelle appeared on stage in a pink leotard and tights, covered with a thin multicolored skirt. The crowd was moved immediately by Michelle's slow spins and her choice of Lionel Richie music. "Hello, is it me you're looking for?" As the routine picked up its pace, the audience began to chant along with Lionel, "Are you somewhere feeling lonely, or is someone loving you?" Now came the moment that my mom had gone over with her several times just before the routine. Wise beyond her years, Michelle had been quite reluctant about my mom's new suggestion. Michelle completed a back handspring and spun around on her hands before backing to the corner of the stage. The music changed abruptly and Kenny Loggins was warning the crowd: "Highway to the danger zone." Michelle stood for a few seconds, snapping and tapping her feet. "Gonna take you right in to the danger zone." My mom was about a foot from Michelle, hiding behind the edge of the curtain. "Now," she whispered to Michelle, who then ripped off her skirt and threw it into the crowd. As she pointed her toe and began her final tumble pass across the stage, my aunt stood up and shouted, "What's the rating on this show?"

Michelle never became a Deanette, mostly because she was indeed a child prodigy and saw things in those girls that the adults didn't seem to notice. Maybe she saw them as a high school harem dressed in pink tights serving prune juice to a woman in pink leg warmers. Or maybe she was that thirty year old boy that decides he's comfortable with the way he ties rope together, and no longer needs a yellow kerchief and a rope tying badge to tell him that he's one damn fine maker of knots. As for the rest of us and our illustrious dance careers, a few months later Miss Helen prodded us into dancing as entertainment in a local Italian street festival. Why was our non-Italian family performing at this public fair? This was about as clear to me as why we were dancing in an Italian festival dressed as Spanish matadors. Miss Helen was so pleased with the festival that she suggested my mom and dad should get involved, and all six of us could begin performing together. Finally and quickly my dad told Ray and I, "Boys, you can quit if you want." And that was it.

Staple

Growing up my brother was known for his curiosity and his low tolerance for pain. Ray would display a keen interest in applying things he saw on television to his real life. And because as little kids we mostly watched cartoons, this became a dangerous habit. Like the time Ray wanted to see if pepper up your nose really makes you sneeze. We all encouraged him to find out. "Go ahead," my mom told him as he snorted lines of black pepper. Nothing happened, so he snorted a few more. After a few minutes, he went on a sort of sneezing frenzy, his head recocking and snapping forward like a shotgun. He covered the dining room with snot, a clear gluey snot with little black speckles in it.

As for his low tolerance for pain, well, we all remember one heated battle at the doctor's office when he was chased throughout the halls and waiting room in an attempt to avoid his shot. It was one of those small doctor's offices in a big white house. The doctor chased Ray first through the office, the waiting room, and then the doctor's upstairs living room and kitchen. As it happened in the middle of the checkup, Ray was wearing only his tighty whities. Finally, sprawled out in his underwear across the doctor's dining room table, my mom held him down and the doctor plunged the needle into Ray's tensed muscles. I on the other hand had a reputation as a tough guy, with a high tolerance for pain. I would roll up my sleeve and ask the doctor for my shot, telling him that I liked getting shots and wished he had more to give me.

One hot summer day, Ray and I returned from the pier where he had been swimming and I had taken a dip. On his way to our family's roast beef stand, my dad had stopped by and dipped me in the water. I had a cast on for most of that summer, and my dad would often hold me by the cast and dip me into the water, so that I could cool off on a hot day. I had won a dirt bike in the swimathon a couple months before, and had taught myself to ride it, but not before breaking my arm. I actually broke it and rebroke it, according to the stunned doctor, by continuing to try to ride my bike with my one strong arm. A few days later my mother noticed me eating cereal with my left hand and eventually took me to the doctor.

If my tough guy attitude was a dangerous combination with a high tolerance for pain, so too was Ray's low tolerance for pain an unfortunate partner for his curiosity. We walked back home from the pier and collapsed on the patio, two skinny shirtless kids resting under a lazy heat. We were home alone for a few hours, my mother out at gymnastics with my sisters. I sat watching my shorts dry, then watched Ray look around the house for distractions. He found our office supply section of the kitchen, a small corner of a corner table that my dad called his office. He bent a few paper clips into triangles and called them different animals, then picked up a stapler and observed it like mammoth bones on the Discovery Channel. He opened it up and considered its inner workings, let the rows of staples slide along with the spring. Then he popped the button to make the stapler lay in one long line and touched the head of it to his thumb. The little points of the next staple stuck out like a snake's fangs which poked at his thumb.

"What are you doing?" I asked him.

"Nothing . . . nothing." He reacted like I had caught him looking at porn. He turned his back to me and pressed the stapler against his thumb, wondering how much pressure you really needed to send the staple flying out of its holder. "I wonder if you can press it just hard enough so that the staple comes out, but pull back quick enough so that it just staples to itself and falls to the ground."

"Ah, you're trying to staple a staple to itself. That's deep." I thought about stopping him. "Yeah, I bet you could do it, but you'd have to be pretty quick."

Ray thought he could press the head quick, and watch the newly formed staple fall to the floor. "Aahhhhhh, mother daaaahhrrr!" Apparently not. He looked up at me and held his thumb high above the other fingers, then headed out to the patio and paced in a circle of fear, holding his thumb high and screaming like some sacred ritual of the stapled thumb.

I thought about calling someone, then remembered my mom's half hour on the phone with the doctor's office when I needed a couple staples removed. They were medical staples, an alternative to stitches, that the doctor had put into my head after an accident at the playground. The receptionist, and then a nurse kept asking my mom, *Now how exactly did your son get staples in his head? You put them there* my mom insisted, which compounded the confusion. Besides, we lived on a dead end road with a lot of friendly neighbors, so we took to the streets.

I led a parade across the yard, followed by Ray's outstretched thumb which was followed by a hollering Ray. We arrived first at the nearest neighbor, the Holders, and found them as usual around the back playing horseshoes. The clink clink of their games filled the summer evenings like chimes, playing most evenings for four or five hours or until the beer ran out. Ray walked over to the youngest of the Holders. The Holders were three sons and their dad, all of them skinny and shirtless like us, except the youngest was thirty-one with a long mustache. He stuck a beer can to the mustache and peered down at Ray's thumb. "Hell, you guys are trying to hitch a ride, eh?" He looked unimpressed, probably having wandered shirtless on our street trying to hitch a ride many times himself.

"Look at my thumb," Ray pleaded.

"Yup, I hear ya baby. But my truck's asleep and I'm whoopin daddy at the shoes, can't leave just now. You keep that thumb a wavin and you guys will catch a ride. Rock on." The two older brothers looked at Ray and gave him a thumbs up in response to his.

I pulled Ray aside and headed to another neighbor's house. The Holders had distracted him a bit, and I took the chance to get a closer look at the little hitchhiker thumb. One side of the staple didn't look that bad, like a staple bent and falling out of a forty page manuscript. The other side was the kind of staple you see in a two page document, imbedded and secure the way a staple was meant to be, well except for its location in my brother's thumb. We both stared at the thumb and then Ray began to lead our parade, sticking it high in the air and screaming down the street.

Our next try was an empty house, followed by a stop at Miss Johnson's summer cottage. Miss Johnson is an elderly woman that didn't want to touch the thumb, but invited us in for cookies. I translated Ray's continued howling as no thankyou, and we continued down the street. Later some of my aunts would claim that Miss Johnson's lack of help was related to a property line dispute between her and one of our second cousins. Running out of options, we wandered off the main street to Mr. Kimball's house, nestled between the woods and a grassy field. We hadn't seen him since we broke his window playing kickball the summer before, then took off, and later were forced to return and apologize. He rocked on the porch in a tall chair. "Aren't you quite a pair. One with a broken arm and the other with a stapled thumb. How'd the other guy fare?"

"Huh?" Ray's hysterics turned confused and then calm.

"My brother got a staple in his thumb," I explained.

"That I can see. Got in a fight with a mean secretary, vicious office assistant?" Mr. Kimball chuckled.

"I stapled my thumb," Ray explained.

The old man stepped into his tool shed and returned with a rusty fishing knife. "Here's my trusty staple remover." He pried the staple out of Ray's hand without too much damage. "That's better."

"Thanks." Ray was relieved to be unstapled. We both looked at his thumb, which now had a deep nick but wasn't bleeding.

"It was a puncture wound, so you don't even bleed at all. You two be careful now, stay outta trouble. Maybe even throw some shirts on, or you'll end up pitchin shoes all day like the Holder boys."

We headed back toward the house, stopping by Miss Johnson, who now claimed to have eaten all the cookies she offered us earlier. Damn property line politics. Stupid second cousins.

Ray stared intently at his shiny red thumb hole, quieted now by the wound. "I wonder."

"What?" I asked.

"I wonder how deep you can cut yourself, if you do it right, without making it bleed."

Violence

I wouldn't say my mother was a violent person, she just had an academic interest in torture and pain. She would somehow convince us to forego traditional medical treatment in favor of slow, painful home remedies. She eventually became a biology and chemistry teacher, but when we were young she relied more on instinct for her cures. My brother Ray's ear infection became an opportunity to excavate with oils and tweezers. For months we would gather downstairs during her nightly dig into my brother's ear. The moaning trickled down from my mom's bedroom/laboratory, and always in the same pattern. Ray would start with a long soft "Owwwwwwe, owwwwe, owwwe," and fade into quicker, monkey-like "Ah, ah, ahhhh." Then after a pause, my mom would say, "Ray, I haven't even touched you yet."

I became entangled in similar experiments when I found out I had a planter's wart on my foot. I realize now that hospitals remove these with ease, a fairly simple procedure. At the time, my mother described that option as a risky surgery leaving an open wound ripe for infection. We turned down the doctor's operation in favor of weeks upstairs with the tweezers. I underwent a similar fate to Ray, except my mom always loved me for my bravery and felt she had more room for experimentation. "I would never try this on your brother, but I think you can handle it." My foot was nightly dug out with the help of eye-drops of acid. The acid was meant to kill the already dead skin of the wart, but I feared as it dripped into the tender recesses of my live skin that perhaps it had designs of it's own. Or maybe my mom's current experiment went beyond the treatment of my foot.

My mom referred to all this as scientific curiosity, a convenient way of excusing sadistic behavior. She passed onto us a sort of delight at the sounds of pain. We began to wait in expectation for the long moans of "owwwe, owwwwee, owwwe, ah ah." No need for TV when you have the comic stylings of child torture echoing throughout the house. Home video contests are usually won with clips of dad's getting baseballs and bike helmets rammed into their balls. In the same comic vein, our family always appreciated the slapstick humor of my dad tripping or bumping his head. Our basement was built on a giant rock. Crawling around to the basement freezer or washing machine was always treacherous. It was not uncommon to hear my dad wack his head on a pipe while switching the laundry, followed upstairs by the canned laughter of a sitcom. We would hear a clang, then "Ahhh shit," and after a moment, "I'm glad you think this is real funny." And we did.

Outside of the family, my mom seemed to kind of ignore the violence around her. Perhaps it just wasn't as interesting when a stranger got tortured or whacked his head. She seemed indifferent to ideas of censoring violence, concerned only with the sexual content and vulgar language that filtered to her young kids. One day when my dad was out at track practice, my mom brought us to the video store. A skinny, self-proclaimed film critic from behind the counter recommended *Angel Heart* to my mom. "But it's rated NC-17," she replied. "Is there a lot of sex and bad language in it, or is it just violence?"

"Mostly just violence," he snapped back, apparently having never watched the long, bloody sex scenes. He looked about sixteen, and maybe his job behind the counter wasn't enough privilege to get those sought after NC-17 rentals.

"Are you sure there's not too much sex and bad words?" continued my mom, concerned for the level of adult material she was about to show her children. "Just lots of regular violence, right?"

"Yup. A lot of people are talking about that one. All the NC-17 movies are pretty good." He smiled and I could see a mustache trying to sprout along his upper lip.

We got about halfway through the movie when my dad walked in. Now my dad was more concerned with the effects of violence on children. Perhaps he felt it built a scar inside them, like the one on his forehead in the shape of our water pipe. He had spent several years in the Air Force after college as part of the ROTC scholarship program. My dad called that branch of the services the "chairforce," because he spent most of his time behind a desk, and bowling and golfing with the other guys on the base. He was always anti-violence and he emerged from the service feeling no different. Growing up we were not allowed to play with toy guns of any kind. While the neighborhood kids shot at us with large water guns, we chased them around with yogurt containers full of water. When they blasted us with cap guns, Ray and I would crouch in the street smashing stacks of caps with a rock, then pointing our finger and yelling *you're dead*.

My dad walked in during the most questionable scene in the whole movie, where Mickey Rourke and that Cosby show girl are fucking in a pile of chicken blood. My dad is a high school history teacher, and his liberal ideas connected the violence of our society with root causes from kid's playtime to pop-warner football. My mother, however, saw no connection between bloody fights on film and the real violence in the world around us. Had the bloody fucking, chicken orgy scene of *Angel Heart* been reduced to a mere bloody cock fight that spills over into the crowd, there would have been no call for my mom's censorship. But Mickey Rourke had to get his bare ass into the mix and so both of my parents stepped in to stop the tape.

"What the hell are you guys watching?" my dad asked all of us.

We shrugged our shoulders and my mom spoke up in our defense. "That's really the worst of it. The rest of the NC-17 stuff was pretty much just violence and a little freaky voodoo stuff. Oh, and honey, you should really watch your language around the kids."

A few weeks later my parents had a rare night out without us kids. My mom suggested that a movie about the civil war couldn't possibly be that risqué, but my dad insisted on leaving us home with a baby-sitter. It was a civil war epic, multiple hours of battles and speeches about honor and men, and men of honor. My mom grew restless and began asking lots of historical questions like, "Doesn't that guy remind you of Uncle Jack?" and "Who's team is he on, anyway?" A big, thick guy two rows in front of them started shushing her, and then turned around and asked her to be quiet. Though my dad I'm sure shared the guy's point if view, my mom quickly gathered him onto her side. She let the man know that her husband was a history teacher, and she could talk to him all she wants. Then she added, that if he had a problem with that he could take it up with my dad. The talk escalated, and the guy suggested that he might stand up, and go outside. "Go ahead, stand up," my mom shouted, as she was not real interested in the movie anyway. "Go outside, who cares, go ahead."

My dad leaned over and tried to calm my mom, "Honey, leave it alone."

She shrugged, "What do I care if he wants to stand up or go outside."

"Honey, that means he wants to fight me."

The big guy stood up, flexed a little, and sat down again. By the end of the film, the audience was in that post-Kevin-Costner-epic type of exhaustion that drowns out any former plans of crushing a history teacher's head into the popcorn machine. My parents came home and told us brave tales of blue fighting grey, and my mom's inadvertent attempts to get my dad's ass kicked. "Well, you could've come with us," she said emphatically, "the whole movie was just violence."

Poor man's

Anyone who has ever shopped in Chinatown understands the concept of the knockoff -- taking home Pumo sweats and Addidaz sneakers. Maybe then you throw on your new sweat outfit, pick some flowers from a neighbor's yard, and show up at your girl's house with the second cheapest wine they had in the store. The rule of second cheapest is important if you have to keep on a budget but you want to show a little class. You bring over the second cheapest box of wine, or tell your lady it's OK for her to order the second cheapest glass of wine off a menu.

But knockoffs and discount substitutes are not limited to sportswear and booze. Often expensive people can be replaced with cheaper versions, like dating a low budget twin of your ex-girlfriend. Hollywood uses this technique, scaling down costs by employing low budget knockoffs of celebrity actors. You may be familiar with the idea of some home brew being the poor man's scotch, or calling a local beach the poor man's Hawaii. But have you noticed, for instance, the poor man's Pacino. You may have a passing thought as you stumble upon a late night movie on TNT or the USA Network, *is that Pacino?* Well, he's short, same feathered hair and he's definitely screaming and sweating like Pacino, but it's not him. You're watching a cheap copy, a man paid to act and sweat and yell in Pacino fashion, the poor man's Pacino. For a moment he could almost pass as Pacino, with his mannerisms, looks, acting style. But wait, the sweat -- yes he's sweating profusely, but not quite as much as Pacino. Nobody sweats on camera like Pacino.

Then there are actors that seem to have made a career out of filling in the roles where a larger star was obviously intended. They have become minor household names in their own right, substitute celebrities. They are knockoffs with their own small following. Nick Nolte has two of these men living in his shadow: Rutger Hauer and Gary Busey. They are three available large, white-haired brutes that pace the room, yell and then fall into tender moments. When a director cannot afford Nick Nolte, he can pace the streets looking for a white-haired brute, or can spend a little more and pick up Rutger Hauer or Gary Busey. They are the second cheapest. They are the poor man's Nick Nolte.

The other day I saw something almost unbelievable. Was that Steve Guttenberg? It looked like him, with the curly hair and the wiseguy smile. But it was an early nineties knockoff, a cheaper version when he was in his glory of *Three Men and a Baby* and eighteen or so *Police Academy* movies. A poor man's Steve Guttenberg – shocking. These days I think he may revive his career as a poor man's Tom Hanks.

Some celebrities can rise up from a poor man's knockoff to a legitimate identity and then fall back again. Of course there are a few exceptions: no matter how famous they might get, people like Gilbert Gottfried or Carrot Top will always be a poor man's version of themselves.

Hand-me-downs

Having twelve daughters certainly minimized my grandmother's interest in fashion. She hand-made most of the clothes they wore, and outfits were rationed out like military uniforms. They each had one dress for special occasions, one towel, one bathing suit, and two casual outfits. On Halloween, my Nana handed out twelve giant paper trash bags, called cleaner bags. The girls were told to draw whatever costume they wanted on the front of it. Every Halloween they dressed as a dozen scribbled on cleaner bags, or white trash.

Their school clothes were simple and modest. Self-expression was left up to the more rebellious girls, like my aunt Sandra. Sandra used to change into more revealing outfits in the bushes at the bottom of the long driveway, just out of sight of the house. She would borrow clothes from friends at school, leaving them in the mailbox in a brown paper bag. In the morning Sandra would change outfits, leaving her clothes in the mailbox, then return home to change back before bringing the mail in. One day my grandfather was home sick from work, and wandered down the hill to get the mail. He opened a brown bag and called up to my Nana, "Honey, one of the girls went to school naked!"

These days my grandmother has developed a stronger interest in the changing fashions, often engaging in long discourses about the genius of Kulats – Cool lots – a shorts/skirt hybrid that still dominates her wardrobe.

My mom carried on my grandmother's legacy, needing only a couple of outfits and some sweats or a robe for laundry day. My dad buys a pair of pants every couple of years, and always the same pair of khakis. He thinks that jeans are a rough and uncomfortable fabric, and his casual clothes are worn out versions of dress clothes. My dad spends long hours weeding his yard, dressed in a bleach-stained collared shirt, cracking leather loafers, and fading khakis with holes.

Growing up we rarely went shopping for clothes. My older sister Michelle was the first one to beg to go shopping for school clothes, finding the middle school crowd unimpressed with her retro look. After months of pleading, my mom finally agreed. Michelle took a shower, chose her least conspicuous outfit, and fixed her hair. She looked in the mirror considering a new hairstyle, dreaming of Guess jeans with extra zippers and turquoise parachute pants. She grabbed a jacket and waited by the door.

My mom called from upstairs, "Michelle, gimme a hand up here."

My mom was wrestling trash bags down the ladder from the attic. "Here, grab these." They rolled a few overstuffed trash bags down the stairs and stacked them together in the living room. She turned to Michelle, "You ready?"

Michelle headed for the door.

My mom ripped open a trash bag -- pastel sweaters and Members Only jackets littered the floor. "We just got this shipment in from aunt Jane. Let's go school shopping." She laughed and played in the outdated fashions like a pile of leaves.

My mom later claimed that "going shopping" was an expression for digging through attic hand-me downs. Michelle disagrees.

"Yeah, this is school shopping," my mom calmly insisted. It was not unlike the time she told Michelle that if she sang loud and hard enough, eventually the church choir would notice her talent and pick her out to join their ranks. Michelle spent the next couple of years belting out loud, emotional renditions of such classics as *Though the Mountains May Fall* and *Eagles Wings* – the Catholic church's answer to *Wind Beneath my Wings*. But the church choir proved an impenetrable club, and her diva performances went unnoticed, outside of the few older women who had asked her to sing more quietly. Years later, she asked my mom again about the church choir. "How often do they pick people for the choir?"

"Pick people?" my mom laughed. "You just show up to choir practice a half hour before the service."

But Michelle did eventually go school shopping, buying new clothes for high school. Unfortunately, by the time she got her hands on Guess jeans and turquoise parachute pants, their popularity was confined to 80s throwback parties and VH-1 rockumentaries.

My brother Ray and I were relatively unaffected by the fashion tragedy of our family. As far as we were concerned, stonewashed jeans and sleeveless sweatshirts were timeless. I do remember our first trip together for a legitimate day of school clothes shopping. Ray and I would both be attending St. John's, a private high school that my parents taught at and therefore we would attend for free. St. John's had a dress code, basically in sync with my dad's usual dress -- a collared shirt tucked into khakis, no jean's allowed.

My mom brought Ray and I to Marshall's, which was having a back to school sale. Down in the basement of the store, we found a small section that apparently was a sale within the sale. A big plastic sign hung over a rack of shirts: Irregular Sale. Indeed it was – the whole rack of shirts was selling for 99 cents a piece. Irregular – we took it to mean unusually low prices, an unusual sale. As it turns out the shirts were just that, unusual -- some had an unusual number of buttons compared to button holes, or one sleeve that was unusually long. And all of the shirts were clearly unusual and irregular in pattern and style: bright plaids, exploding flowery designs, Hawaiian shirts with striped collars.

Marshall's was pawning off their production mistakes as merchandise. We laughed and tried on misprinted shirts with odd dimensions. But Ray and I were accustomed to wearing ugly patterns and ill-fitting clothes. We bought all of the shirts off the rack, eight each. Sixteen shirts for under twenty dollars – we were set for the upcoming school year, and the joke was on Marshall's.

27

We lived year round on a street filled mostly with summer cottages, but we vacationed in New Hampshire. Actually, people with money *vacation*, we just went on vacation. And expensive getaways always carry their own definite articles, like *the* islands, or more specifically *the* Poconos. Near us, rich people vacationed on *the* Cape and *the* Vineyard, places we knew as Cape Cod and Martha's Vineyard. Someone would tell you, *oh I always vacation on the Vineyard*, where one of my aunts would tell you, *we took a ferry to Martha's Vineyard; those houses are friggan huge*. Most years we spent a week at my aunt Nancee's house in New Hampshire, where we vacationed at *the* mini golf courses, *the* water slides, and battled *the* horseflies.

Some days my uncle would get us free passes for the waterslides at the ski mountain. Other days we would hike in the mountains, float in tubes down the river, or search the woods for dead animals. At night we would sit outside by the river around a campfire. We told ghost stories and roasted marshmallows, but my mom and aunt Nancee were otherwise occupied. They would sit just off to the side, whispering, plotting. Nancee would nod to my mom, and she would begin. "Alright kids, what do you want to do tomorrow?"

We responded with shouts of I dunno, mini golf, ice cream, swimming.

"Who said I dunno? Julie?"

Julie wrinkled her face and thought hard. "I wanna find dead rats."

My mom took it all in, like an improv performer taking suggestions from the audience. "Alright I heard dead rats. And mini golf, swimming, and ice cream."

My mom and aunt Nancee would huddle together, talking fast and high pitched like midgets in Disney and David Lynch movies. We overheard some of the key points in the plan: *we might want to space out the swimming and the ice cream . . . somehow put a little time between the ice cream and the dead rats . . . let's think about this in another way, dead rats is to swimming as ice cream is to what? Oh, minigolf – perfect.* One of them would giggle and they would rush into the kitchen, covering the table with brochures, coupons, an atlas. They consulted road maps, then threw them aside and drew their own maps with a stick in the dirt.

After a long session of strategic planning, mom and Nancee came to the campfire to debrief. They would return with the plan, which was always a series of possible plans. Aunt Nancee would identify the plans by letters, like evidence in court. "Well kids, we currently have three distinct plans, though they overlap some, that we'll call plan a, plan b, and plan c." We waited through the lengthy descriptions, knowing that the real plan was never any of the ones initially presented.

Then my mom always came in with a darkhorse plan. "All three plans are solid, full day itineraries. But what I might suggest is a plan d, a sort of combination of a and c, with the spirit and atmosphere of plan b."

We smiled as Nancee rose to her feet. "That's nothing short of brilliant." The presentation of the plan was then cut short by an impromptu discussion of past plans. Nancee and my mom began to reminisce about some of the best plans they had made. My aunt Nancee beamed with pride, as my mom remembered Nancee's plan of homemade blueberry pancakes followed by a hike and a swim, and bingo night at the church. Nancee returned the favor with a tale of one of my mom's best plans, where she had combined a bacon and egg breakfast with some local pig races, squeezed in two theme parks that were having free promotional days, and wound up making candles at a nudist open house. They began to discuss the best plan ever laid by either of them, as each mother hen had hatched her share of great plans. The discussion became it's own mini planning session, concerned with how overcoming obstacles or the total price of a well-planned day would effect the rankings. They giggled and told stories late into that night around the campfire, tales of picnics during thunderstorms and five day vacations for six for just under seven dollars a head. By the morning, they were still the first two awake, drawing homemade maps that would make AAA blush and figuring out the best way to pack the cooler.

Our last trip to New Hampshire brought my mom together with her eleven sisters, probably the most daring and edgy plan in years. We were celebrating my grandparent's 50th wedding anniversary. As most of the twelve girls have three to five kids, we basically took over a motel for the weekend. The few rooms that were left were soon vacated, some people just leaving their belongings and running barefoot down the street. We are a loud and energetic bunch. The motel manager handed us the keys for the weekend and asked us not to break anything that looked real expensive.

The twelve girls quickly set up camp around the motel, conforming the amenities to their own use. The lobby was covered with signs and schedules like Club Med, mostly food related information like scheduled snack times. The pool area became a watersports arena, filled with styrofoam noodles and nerf balls. It was like a cross between synchronized swimming and American Gladiators – a group of cousins performed water shows, while another crew of wet, skinny cousins beat them with long styrofoam weapons.

The brunch area was transformed into a talent show, cousins wandering up to sing songs, tell jokes, or make farting sounds with unusual parts of their body. The most strange and artsy piece came from my five year old cousin Tommy, who just sat grunting, letting the audience become his show like a deep performance artist. "He's doing a lucky," one of my aunts yelled out, which is a slang term for taking a crap that came from a little cousin who couldn't pronounce yucky. Undisturbed, Tommy continued silently making strained faces, tensing his brow and curling his lips. "He's playing with himself," another aunt yelled out in support. After another few minutes, Tommy addressed the crowd, softly and almost in a question, "My whole act is thinking." Then about fifty voices echoed his line, "His whole act is thinking." And then we thought about it, too. It provided a rare moment of introspection in the carnival of our family reunion. The silence was soon broken by our self-proclaimed emcee, Aunt Brenda, "I really thought he was playing with himself. Who's next?"

The weekend went along fairly smoothly. As one of the older cousins, I was able to stay mostly out of danger. I stayed away from any heated discussions of the plan, left the room when a husband was accused of not pitching in, and didn't go near the shuffleboard which had been converted into a homemade skeet shoot area. Someone would throw a ceramic disk into the air and the shooter would hurl the pole at it. Of course with over thirty cousins running wild, I would receive the occasional kick in the kidneys or punch in the balls, usually followed by *what's your name anyway?*, or *are you my cousin?*

Though it was rare to see anything interrupt a Chalifour girls' schedule of events, news arrived that the nearby waterpark was having a special. Discounts, freebies, and bargains -- this was the glue that held a clan of twelve girls together. Grampy couldn't have been more proud on his 50th wedding anniversary than seeing his twelve girls unite around a good deal. This one day promotion was a price per car instead of per person at the Whale's Tail waterpark. Not only was this an obvious deal, but a complex riddle for the girls to sink their teeth into. Factions of sisters broke into various committees, one in charge of picking the car that could fit the maximum passengers, another considering the body types and sizes of everyone like a tetris game. My dad's minivan was chosen, and after some consideration the two back seats were removed. Cousins, uncles, and later aunts lined up and were chosen by body type for specific sections of the car. Aunt Nancee and my mom headed to the front of the line and began choosing passengers. Aunt Nancee studied the van, "Hey, we could put a big person here, as long as they are big in the back but small up front."

The command got passed down like a game of telephone and then my mom yelled out, "We need a big ass with no boobs."

"That's a lot of us," one of my aunts yelled back, which got a big laugh from the crowd and then a stern warning about staying on task.

The larger people were put in first as a foundation, and some of the tiny cousins would be sprinkled in as filler, like pebbles. We all began to laugh about places to fit some of our smallest cousins. Perhaps it was the joy of family, or the heat and sweat of bodies stacked high on top of us in a minivan. We became giddy and faint. Hey, stick her in the ashtray. I think we can fit those two in the glove compartment. My mom perked up, "Good idea. Open the glove compartment."

Aunt Nancee was always right behind her. "Oh yeah, great minds think alike. If we open the glove compartment, uncle Jack can stick his elbow in there and that'll leave enough room on his chest for Kathy's baby. Perfect."

My mom's eyes met Aunt Nancee's. "What a rush. It's so great when it all comes together."

My mom and Nancee were the last to fit in. The last two spaces in the car were cut outs of their bodies. The sliding door shut with skin pressed against every part of it. My dad sat at the wheel, "This is gonna be tough driving with two kids in my lap."

"Oh please," my mom said. "It's only two miles."

As we pulled into the driveway of the waterpark, a smiling whale pointed to a wooden sign that read, The Whale's Tail: A Family Run Water Park. I can't be sure if someone had spray painted a word onto it, or if the heat and collective body sweat was fueling my imagination. I read the sign as, The Whale's Tail: A Family Run-Down Water Park. And indeed it was. Corroding paper mache whales scared the little cousins, while creaky, rusty waterslides scared the rest of us. But pulling into their driveway was its own reward. A pimply high school kid peered into the van and then ran for the other employees and a camera. "Holy shit, how many you got in there?"

A voice came from deep beneath piles of skinny cousins, beaming with pride. "We got twenty seven. These are my twelve girls and their families. Did you ever see so many in one car before?"

The whale's tale employee of the month smiled and snapped a picture in the direction of Grampy's voice. The picture would just be a stack of arms and legs, looking like the aftermath of a collapsed slide and probably never finding it's way into the brochures. "No shit," he laughed. "I think the record before was nine."

"Well, thanks girls," Grampy muttered under some cousins.

"Happy 50th!" we all yelled, or those of us that had our mouths uncovered.

Another voice came from deep in the pile. "Now let's get the hell outta this car. Little Tommy appears to be in a little trouble, unless his whole act is fainting."

Kelly's

While my mom's father was famous for making girls, my dad's father gained fame making roast beef sandwiches. If you read the paper placemat or the side of a take-out bag, you'll see that my grandfather and his friend hit the beach over fifty years ago with a cooked roast beef and a loaf of bread. That was the origin of Kelly's Roast Beef, a roast beef and seafood stand that's been our family business ever since. They built it up on the first public beach in the United States, where my great grandmother was the first woman to wear a bathing suit: Revere Beach. My great grandfather was the husband of this controversial lady, clad in a skimpy bathing suit that went down almost to her knees. He was also the mayor of Revere for many years.

Both of my dad's parents grew up about a mile from the strip, when Revere Beach was a hot spot for celebrity performers and socialites. My Nana tells stories of jazz legends and glamorous parties down by the beach. When my dad was growing up, Revere Beach had begun to lose a little of the glitz, falling from its Atlantic City lure to an amusement ride boardwalk. It became a place to take your family instead of your mistress. Kelly's grew with the changing crowd, pushing hot roast beef sandwiches and deep fried seafood out of twelve take-out windows.

My dad remembers the carnival rides, the games, and especially the Cyclone roller coaster. My dad's brother Kevin worked on a documentary about the old days of Revere Beach. They interviewed my grandfather about Kelly's, and showed the changing landscape of the beach from lively nightclubs to family boardwalk to condos. My favorite part of the documentary was an interview with one of the Hurley's, a local family that had run the Cyclone roller-coaster for years. He stood with his thumbs in his pants, looking off toward the water. "What? Oh, the deaths. Yeah, people like to make a big deal about that sort of thing, it really wasn't that big a deal. Listen, if you're gonna be in the roller coaster business for a number of years, some people are gonna die. It's simple arithmetic."

By the time I came around, the glitzy days of Revere Beach and the amusements rides of the boardwalk were only stories for the holidays, and framed black and white pictures at my grandparents' house. The main attractions now at Revere Beach were Kelly's Roast Beef, and of course the beach itself. Kelly's had grown in popularity as the attractions around it had faded, leaving a strip of condos along the beach towering over one small roast beef stand. Kelly's began to have a scene of its own. Throughout the years Kelly's had a stream of devoted fans, willing to wait in the rain for clam chowder, or standing in the snow to get a hot roast beef sandwich. During the summer, the beach was crowded with families and teenagers, overflowing the extended sidewalk in front of Kelly's waiting for their clam roll or seven hotdogs.

But it was the summer night crowd that really gave Kelly's and Revere Beach it's reputation. Ask my Nana about Revere Beach and she'll tell you stories about Lena Horne and Charlie Parker, or her husband spending long nights trying to get a business started. Ask any kid born on the north side of

Boston in the 70s or 80s about Revere Beach and he'll conjure up images of beefy guys in tank tops and gold chains chasing girls down the street with giant hair-sprayed hairdos. Yeah, if you're not real familiar with the east coast, just think of New Jersey and that'll get you started.

When I was in high school, my favorite radio station was WBCN, *the rock of Boston*. They played a lot of Aerosmith, Led Zeppelin, AC/DC, thrown in with the softer stuff like Winger or that Cinnamon Girl song. The station came out with a spoof of Vanilla Ice's big hit at the time -- *ice ice baby, ding ding ding ding di di ding ding* -- which is really a spoof all by itself. It played constantly on the radio for about six months, and it was all about the Revere Beach crowd outside of Kelly's. It only had one verse which went like this: *Hanging out Revere Beach sitting on the wall, checking out the bitches drinking PBR talls, my other hand is free so I tug on my balls, baby. . . go guido, go guido, go . . . ding ding ding ding di di ding ding . . . go guido go guido go . . . ding ding ding ding di di ding ding.*

That's the soundtrack for the nighttime Kelly's crowd. Kelly's was across the street from a long strip of parking spots that butted up against a low wall on the edge of the beach. Lots of cars spent the night cruising up and down the strip, but the heavy portion of the crowd came early and claimed their parking spots across from Kelly's. They would open their trunks and show off their car stereos, sitting on the wall waiting for a girl who was impressed by a big bass tube. There were all kinds of folks coming down to Kelly's at night. But mostly the crowds separated themselves like a high school cafeteria. One area was always lined with Harley bikes and the leather clad . . . some rockers . . . but the real icon of the summer nights on Revere Beach was what the Vanilla Ice cover referred to, the guidos. *Hanging out revere beach sitting on the wall.* These guys wore tight jeans with a white tank top, maybe covered by a shiny black leather jacket, and definitely covered by a bucket of musky cologne. Then there were the ones who got more dressed up, purple Z Cavarichis and a puffy white shirt -- but always with a nice gold chain, and maybe a little dangler in the shape of a twisted sharks tooth or the playboy symbol. They spent more money on their stereos than the cars that housed them, and they stood by the back of the car pumping some top 40 tune like Tone Loc, mouthing the words as girls passed by, "I like to do the wild thing."

Checking out the bitches drinking PBR talls. The wall was lined with tough girls that teased the boys almost as much as they teased their hair. There were two main approaches, volume and isolation: volume was the all out can and a half of hairspray lion's mane, stretching and reaching to show the boys as much hair as possible; isolation was a more subtle approach that really showed off the girl's skill as well as her hair, spraying up particular portions and leaving other parts flat. When I met my high school sweetheart she had a simple flat hairdo, with a four inch wide, thin wall of hair that stuck straight up from her forehead. I met her at a football game, and she showed me a slice in her ear, where another girl outside of Kelly's had ripped her earring out. And I was hooked. Yes the girls were out there, drinking their *PBR talls*, Pabst Blue Ribbon tall bottles.

Revere Beach had the music, the ocean, the food, plenty of atmosphere. All that was left was for the guys to seduce themselves a little guidette. *My other hand is free so I tug on my balls.* Like the song says, they would grab their crotches, and not just scratch at their balls like a guy watching the football game, or a baseball player. You had to grab your balls with a quick tugging motion which punctuated what you were saying as you did it -- like "Hey, or I got two orders of scallops over here baby" or "Hey, wanna piece of this." In most places in the world this interaction would end badly. Here the girls would respond "Yeah sure, I'll get a piece of that if that's your stereo that's bumpin Tone Loc," or one would turn to her friend, "Oh shit girl, they got scallops over there, they're expensive, I bet these guys are rich."

So nights out at Revere Beach were worthy of a jingle, which actually sounds more like this when it's sung right: *Hangin out Reveah Beach sittin on da wall, checkin out da bitches drinkin PBR tawls, my odda hand is free so I tug on my bawls, baby. . . go guido, go guido, go . . .* And well, if they couldn't get girls, the guys could always get into fights with each other, and usually did. Either way, they got delicious food from Kelly's, so it was a good night all around. *Fuckin A!*

Cheese Stacker

The sign reads *Kelly's Roast Beef: Famous the World Over*. Our slogan was validated the day my family found someone using a Kelly's paper cup in Tijuana. The sign has a shamrock instead of an apostrophe and a big fat guy chopping roast beef. The popular beach front stand features twelve take-out windows and no inside space for customers, though it's the inside of Kelly's that really gives the place character.

Local legends spent long hours making onion rings and deep frying hand-breaded scallops and clams. Like a soap opera, many of the characters started out slicing roast beef and were written off the show with strange plot twists. Like the guy that left for LA to pursue a film career and found work in the porn industry, or the grill guy, our hot dog and burger specialist, who stumbled upon the idea of selling water in the desert. Both found their way back into the script like TV actors that never made their break into film. The porn star came back to work the deep fryer and our grill guy discovered they already had ample suppliers of water to Las Vegas.

Kelly's was full of colorful personalities. Almost as interesting and usually more dramatic were the stories that customers made up. "Hey, I'm the owner's son. I'm supposed to pick up some free stuff."

"Oh really." Someone would yell back to my dad or my uncle. "You might want to come up here, this guy says he's your brother."

Or there were always the folks that were convinced that last week they bought something that is now not on the menu. "I'll get a seafood combo platter and some mozzarella sticks."

"Sorry, we don't have combo plates or mozzarella sticks."

The giant menu loomed overhead, combo platters and mozzarella sticks nowhere to be seen. "Don't be ridiculous, I've been buying combo platters from here every Sunday for the past two years."

"Interesting."

Customers told tales of bags of cash hidden in the back, and scandalous stories about the owners and the old days of Kelly's. Rarely did they realize that they were talking to the owner's son or grandson, who was just taking it all in. Like the young girl working next to me one summer, that told me that the family of the owners didn't work at all, and that she was pretty sure they all lived in Florida because that's where rich people live.

I had grown up with stories of wild summer nights at the beach -- the fights, the cops, the girls. I remembered my uncle Kevin's infamous first night working at Kelly's. A drunk customer ordered a meatball sub, something that has never been a part of the menu at Kelly's. The guy mistook my uncle's confusion for rudeness and pulled him over the counter by the shirt. A couple of employees grabbed Kevin's skinny legs and dragged him back through the take-out window. They gave the guy a roast beef sandwich and he was satisfied. He took a bite, "Yeah, now this is a fuckin meatball sub," and staggered off. An hour later a famous disk jockey came to the window – the Wolfman. His date wore a tight pink halter top. She approached the counter and pulled her top down to her waist, like a little pink belt, and the Wolfman began to howl and bury his beard in her chest. My uncle turned to my dad who had been working there for several years, "Wow, is it always like this? I love Kelly's."

I first worked at Kelly's the summer before I went to St. John's, at the age of fourteen. Kevin's first shift at Kelly's was fresh in my mind as I got dressed for my first day on the job. I put on a new Kelly's T-shirt with jeans and a pair of sneakers, then thought about my dad's Kelly's clothes that smelled of deep fried food and were never allowed in the house. They remained in the cellar, worn khaki pants stiff with dried flour and flour-caked shoes. My dad would hand-batter the seafood, and his dried up pants were just a testament to the rare quality of Kelly's fresh seafood, as he often reminded us.

My mom dropped me off at Kelly's at five in the morning. That first summer I worked an early morning shift, from five a.m. to nine a.m. I wondered who might try to beat me up, and if any girls would be flashing this early. The morning crew was an odd collection of Kelly's employees in semi-retirement, a sort of Kelly's Roast Beef living hall of fame. The old guys welcomed me in as their mascot. There was Sonny, a tall blonde ex-boxer and his short sidekick Peanuts, always by his side with thick-rimmed glasses and hounds-tooth pants. Then there was Howie, considered quite the youngster as he was still in his 60s. He showed me the ropes. The morning work was minimal for the crew we had, but I did almost all the work. The old guys manned the windows, selling an occasional coffee or donut, and entertaining the early bird old men crowd that never missed a morning of Kelly's gossip. Howie taught me all the prep work that needed to be done for the day – filling buckets of pickles, cupping trays of tartar sauce, and my specialty: stacking cheese. I was known as the cheese stacker, and spent most of the morning piling white and yellow slices of American cheese on paper plates, crisscrossing the edges of cheese to make the slices easier for the grill man to grab hold of. The nights at Kelly's were so busy that this was considered a necessary task, to keep the grill from getting backed up with orders.

The morning hours at Kelly's are quiet, but the old guys spent time cracking corny jokes for me. Then I headed outside to rake the trash along the sidewalk, and battle the large, well-fed seagulls. A nasty job with a beautiful view, raking paper plates along the beach as the sun slowly crept into place. I returned inside, just a half hour before the end of my first shift.

Howie called me over. "How's my cheese stacker? Hey, Peanuts cooked you up an egg sandwich. Take a little break."

I asked Howie, "Did you ever get into any fights while you worked here?"

He laughed, and jiggled his growing belly. "With all this fried food in here, what am I gonna do? A big hunk of muscle with a little pinhead on it came to my window the other day, and tried to start something, said he was gonna kick my ass."

I got excited, "What did you do?"

"I just told him, hey, you think you'd be the first guy to kick my ass. You don't think I've had my head pounded in before. Big deal, so you kick my ass." He shrugged. "And the guy kind of lost interest."

Bill came wandering in for a visit, one of the old retired guys that couldn't help hanging around Kelly's in the morning hours. "Hey new kid, check this out." He dropped his pants.

Howie stepped in, "Put it away, Bill. Don't show that thing to my cheese stacker."

"But I got a new unit, it's always semi-erect, and then I got this clever pump over here."

"Hey, whaddya know. That's wonderful. A new semi, huh?"

Sonny and Peanuts were suddenly shouting from the front window. "Go Al, Go." They began to chant in unison with a crowd that had gathered. "Al! Al! Al!"

An old scruffy guy, apparently named Al, was wandering

away from the nearby nursing home, sneaking off in his Johnny. I later learned he had nearly escaped almost a dozen times, always cheered on by the local Kelly's employees. "Al! Al! Al!" they chanted. "Al! Al! Al!" we chanted together. And Al dipped and spun, his light blue Johnny blowing in the breeze behind him. He moved fast enough to escape, just not consistently in one direction. Soon two big brutes in white coats caught up to him. One grabbed Al and rushed him back inside the brick building. The second one lingered outside, flipping off a now jeering crowd of old men, one of them semi-erect, and a young cheese stacker.

Low budget

My dad was a high school teacher that worked summers at the family roast beef stand, and my mom was a part-time waitress. Almost everything we did involved some sort of money saving technique.

What's most scary are the ways we saved money in the kitchen. You know how some guys have many levels of dirty clothes -- *This T-shirt stinks a little, but turn it inside out and it's good for a few days.* That's kind of how my mom was growing up with food that had gone bad. There wasn't just good food and rotten food, there were many subtle levels. Like food that just needed the mold cut off of it. Or worse, meat that was just a little rotten. We would have a couple of big barbecues at the house every year, and we'd get food from the family business like huge boxes of frozen hamburgers and giant containers of ketchup. Then we were forced to eat the leftovers for far too long. Months later, we'd be trying to break apart the hamburgers to make them into something else. Did you ever try to make meatballs from pre-formed frozen hamburgers that are just a little freezer burned?

Mom, this hamburg smells a little funny.

Put a little more oregano in it and its good for a few days.

People in the old days put salt on meat to keep it from going bad. My mom thought she could use spices to bring meat back, that had already crossed over to rotten – she was like the Frankenstein of rotten meat.

Mom, the hamburg looks kind of blue. There were little discolored rainbows in the meatballs, the way they show up in an oil leak.

Oh, don't worry about it, I'm gonna put it in a casserole. Casserole was one if the scariest words around my house, because it meant rotten food hidden among other ingredients in a glass pan.

And we got all of our condiments from the family business, so there were always two sizes to choose from, the tiny packets of ketchup and mustard, and 2 gallon containers. A few months after a big party, the 2 gallon tanks always tasted tangy, no matter what the original flavor was. Extra tangy barbecue sauce was not that bad, but somehow the ketchup was tangy, and the mayo was real tangy. And my parents kept pushing the big containers. I think the little packets of condiments were like our version of a fallout shelter. We didn't have a real basement because the house was built on a huge rock, but what we did have was several brown paper bags filled with tiny nutritional packets of warm mayonnaise and relish. And not just from our family's fast food spot; anytime we ate somewhere where these emergency supplies were kept out in reach, on our way out my mom always said the same thing: *Alright kids, fill your pockets with supplies,* which meant everything from napkins and straws to tiny packets of hot sauce. We couldn't be sure what the future would bring, but if survival had anything to do with tiny packets of spoiled mayonnaise, we would be ready.

My parents tried to make things exciting for us on special occasions, but of course there were some necessary budget cuts here as well. For our friends' birthdays, we didn't have to go to the mall because we had our own gift shop right in the house.

Mom, can't I go to the mall and get Jimmy a frisbee, or a tape of Duran Duran?

No, honey, we have a lot of nice things in the giftshop that would be perfect for Jimmy. Why don't you go take a look?

The giftshop was upstairs in my sisters' room. It was a little plastic box under the bunk beds full of assorted knickknacks and recycled gifts -- actually, it was a washed out fish container from the family roast beef and seafood stand. It was full of things like salt and pepper shakers in the shape of little dogs, a necklace with a butterfly on it, a crystal statue of two fish kissing.

My mom would say, *why don't you give Jimmy that nice statue of the fish?*

Uh, cause he'll think I'm a girl.

Well, why don't you give him that cool chain?

Mom, it's a necklace . . . with a butterfly on it.

No, I think it's kind of manly. It looks more like a moth to me, guys can wear moths, that's tough -- it's like wearing a spider, or a shark's tooth.

On our own birthdays, my parents would try to go all out and throw us a big party. But for many years, to save a few bucks, we didn't have our own birthday parties. We would have one big summer barbecue to celebrate all four of our birthdays. That's where the big cases of hamburger and giant containers of mayonnaise often showed up. It was a special occasion indeed, this was a celebration of eating food before it expired. We would have piñatas outside hanging from a tree -- well, homemade piñatas. My mom would tie a string between two trees, and put balloons along it. Each kid would get a turn with the blindfold on, holding a whiffle bat with a pin taped to the end of it. A couple of the balloons were filled with candy, but most of them just had little pieces of paper with numbers on them. The numbers corresponded to prizes

in the gift shop. *I got a number two; I won two little dogs .
. . and they're salt and pepper shakers . . . great.* Then there
were always a couple balloons that were filled with water, so
that the blindfolded kid would get the prize of being doused
with water -- this was really just entertainment for the adults.

Even the big holidays had a sort of thrifty edge. My
family has always taken their own low budget approach
to the holidays. I guess a lot of it goes back to my mom's
dad, my Grampy, who had twelve girls, and he found every
way he could to save money. For a few weeks around every
Christmas my Grampy would put on the yule log channel; it
was a local cable channel that played a flaming log all day.
He'd put it on, then drop the heat down a couple of notches.
Grampy would sit back in his lazy boy, with his headphones
on so he could hear the warm crackling of the fire, rubbing his
hands together and dreaming of a low gas bill.

My mom carried on his legacy around the holidays.
Halloween costumes were always made up of household stuff.
When I was 8, I wanted to be Rocky.

My mom looked at me, "You wanna be Rocky. Put your
father's blue robe on, and we'll rub a little shoe polish under
your eye. Let's see, we don't have any boxing gloves -- oh,
we'll wrap your hands with medical tape and put a little tangy
ketchup on them, and you'll be Rocky from that scene where
he's pounding the frozen meat."

I was no stranger to trying to break down frozen meat, from
my days with the frozen hamburger patties.

When I was 10, I wanted to be a smurf. My mom looked
me over, "Well, you're already short, so that helps. Um, blue
eye shadow all over your face, and tell your sister to bring in
a pillow case." She placed a white pillow case on my head.
"There ya go, you're a smurf. Who's next?"

The same theme of homemade costumes carried over
from Halloween to Christmas. For our family, Halloween
and Christmas weren't all that different. Every Christmas

we would dress up for mass at the Catholic church. Me, my brother and two sisters were shepherds in the nativity scene, up on the altar at the midnight mass. Most of the other kids wore fancy outfits with brown cloaks and shepherd beards and staffs. Our shepherd gear was basically an odd assortment of robes. I would wear my dad's blue robe, and my sisters would have on a thin pink shiny robe and a yellow robe covered with little daisies. I remember one year my little sister Julie was crying as she pleaded with my mom, "Why does Pat get to dress up like Rocky?" We didn't have those nice rope belts. My sisters wore those stretchy belts with the magnets in the front, and me and Ray had on those striped cardboard belts that come with cheap pants. But mostly we looked fresh out of the spa -- with our bathrobes on, and towels hanging down from our heads. It was like we had casually wandered onto the altar looking for the baby Jesus. *Is Jesus here? Yeah, sorry we're late . . . we just got out of the shower. Is Jesus around here? We brought him a little present – it's a statue of two fish kissing.*

Self-portrait

Dads get socks, razors, ties for gifts. But what do dads really want for gifts? Maybe sunglasses, new car stereos, nudie playing cards. We always bought my dad socks, underwear, handkerchiefs and Nestle's Crunch bars. His holidays were spent lounging in clean white undergarments, eating chocolate.

But more recently, under the guise of getting things for my dad that he really wants, I buy him gag gifts, boxed symbolic jokes tied with ribbon. I've given him pictures of beefcake men in their briefs, in memory of the times he staggers downstairs in his tighty whities telling us and our friends, all in our twenties and thirties now, to go to bed. I gave him a rubber poseable female wrestler that looked like a drag queen, calling it a gender bender, a mascot for the new class he was teaching on gender issues.

Last Christmas I bought him a pair of jeans, a seemingly simple and humorless gift. Not so. My dad has a long history of refusing to wear jeans, and has made many a passionate speech about the uncomfortable fabric that is denim. Casual wear? Hardly. My dad describes jeans as sandpaper pants scratching against his skin. His comfort wear pants are worn out khakis with fancy pleats and little holes around the pockets. "You can't possibly find a pair of pants more comfortable than these," he'll proclaim, "It's like you're not even wearing them at all." He slips on a pair of worn out loafers with the tassels torn off, then crosses the room and rubs the leg of my jeans. "Scratchy, rough, sand paper." He opened his present, we all laughed, and he tried them on. We all took pictures with my dad in his new jeans, memorializing the first and last moment he ever wore them. "You do realize there's no way I'm gonna use these," he said.

This was the new pattern of gifts for my dad. He would open up a present, we would all laugh, and the gift would go unused, the jeans unworn, the beefcake pictures taken down from the mantel, the gender bender left unbent. This Christmas would be different. I resorted back to the old days of gift giving, back before the gag gifts, before the underwear and chocolate, to the days when giving a present meant a little hard work and inspiration. My dad always seemed to love the popsicle stick houses and macaroni necklaces of our earliest Christmasses. I decided that if my dad could still wander downstairs in his briefs and tell my thirty year old girlfriend to go to bed, the least I could do was make him a present.

My girlfriend and I had just moved into a new apartment in San Francisco, on the edge of San Francisco. A three block stroll to the next town over brought you to the Cow Palace, a huge stadium that week to week brought in drastically different crowds for shows like: Motorcross, WWF, religious fanatic conventions, Charles Dickens Christmas Fairs, Harlem Globetrotters, Rodeo, Exotic Erotic Ball, and constant liquidation blowout sales. We would attend computer shows in the wake of rodeos, where skinny pin-striped shirts tried to sell us computer chips in a room full of hay that smelled like horse shit. We would inhale the thick black smoke of the Motorcross shows, dance the Texas two-step with cowboys that wore tighter jeans than their girlfriends, and eat at the local fast food chains with alternating crowds of mormons, rockers, and trekkies.

But at this time we were just unpacking, sifting through boxes of our junk. I snooped and stalked like an outsider, finding personal treasures in old boxes that hadn't been touched in several moves. Old letters, pictures, pocket notes reviving old stories. I came across an old picture of my dad working as a high school track coach. My dad had basic outfits he would wear for many years, and a certain look and stance when he took pictures. So this picture of him was like an icon for that decade. These were the days of my dad's yellow shorts. A legendary pair of shorts, they had shown much of his lower thighs and hugged his small butt for possibly eight years. This picture appeared to be somewhere near the beginning, as the little yellow shorts were still working hard to project an almost blinding yellow. In their later years they would struggle and sag a bit, fading to a white yellow. A long sleeve track T-shirt was tucked into the little stretch waist band. The pocket area read St. John's Track, Catholic Conference Champs, with a couple of years listed along the arm. These shirts were known in my family as The Sleeve, as later shirts had ten or twelve years, conference victories notched along the arm. He wore sneakers with short socks, almost peds, and my family's hereditary calves bursting between the low socks and bright yellow shorts. My dad complained that long socks would choke his calves, another issue he had with jeans.

My dad stood, as he always did, with his hands clasped behind his back, legs apart, hips forward, rocking into a big smirk. This pose was cut and pasted throughout about thirty years of my dad's life. With today's technology, there's no real reason for my dad to take any more pictures. We can use this pose as a basis, then change his outfits, locations and hairline to suit the appropriate memory and mood.

The highlight of my dad's old look was certainly his hair and mustache. He had a decent head of hair, with one strong part from left to right that sagged down in an arc across his forehead. The shape echoed his patented closed mouth grin, that played beneath a thick brown mustache. This was a hearty, tough guy mustache, fully replacing his upper lip. In the 70s his look said tough and sexy, Magnum PI, short shorts with a thick cop mustache. In the 90s it was just as cute, but in a gay porn kind of way.

These days I usually shave my head pretty short, but only every few months or so. I am still rooted in my childhood haircut philosophy. My brother and I were sent to the barber shop about every six months to get our heads shaved. And when the hair began to grow down over our ears and eyes, we would go again. I happened to have pretty long hair and a full beard the day of our move. I found an old bright yellow bathing suit and a long-sleeve track shirt I had taken from my dad. I fished around for a small pair of my girlfriend's socks and then some old yellow and black Saucony running shoes. I wet my head, used a little gel, and made a strong part in my hair across my forehead. I went in the bathroom and came out with a retro make over. My girlfriend screamed then laughed, and I told her to get the camera. I put on the short socks and sneakers. I rolled the yellow shorts around the waist to make them shorter, then tucked the T-shirt into them. And my mustache was perfect. Thick and fatherly, a sexy 70s cop that had traveled twenty years in the future to cruise a biker bar.

I stood in front of a blank white wall. I leaned my hips forward, and clasped my hands behind my back. "Smile," she said, and I made my dad's big smirk. She snapped a picture and leaned back for another. A soft knock at the open door. We greeted our new neighbor, my girlfriend with her camera and me in my huge mustache and tiny yellow shorts. "I don't usually look like this," I tried to explain. "This is what my dad used to look like," I clarified.

Our new neighbor laughed. He welcomed us with his words, but his eyes asked the questions: *Porno? Your dad's in porno?*

That Christmas my dad opened his gifts, sat back in his rocking chair ready for socks and gag gifts, chocolate and jokes. He opened my picture and right away I could tell that this was another inside joke that he would not be part of. He smiled a little, said thanks, then looked at me. "Why did you give me an old picture of myself?"

Chores

Cultures are defined by their habits, language and norms; sometimes a culture is confined to a small section of society, a tiny subcommunity, like a household. As we grew older, my siblings and I slowly realized the culture of our house was very different from the outside world. It was like finding out that the Vatican is it's own country, or the first time I saw Luxemborg on a map. We were a tiny overlooked dot, easily mistaken as a smudge or a spot of drool.

One of the most obvious signs of cultural difference is language. Our language was a slightly recognizable perversion of a more widespread dialect -- English. Much of the language derived from the ancient tribe that was my mother's family, an historically misunderstood clan of twelve daughters and their breeders. We had our own patterns of speech, the way that other people say *please* and *thank you*. The statement that someone was sick, for instance, was always followed by the question, *Did you get sick?* The emphasis was on the word *get*. Just as please is a gentler way to say get me that, did you get sick was a polite way of getting right to the crucial information, translating roughly as *Was there throwup involved?* There were new words that developed into new expressions. Like the word lucky became a synonym for poop, after my little cousin repeatedly pointed to a diaper yelling *lucky lucky* in an attempt to call the diaper yucky. The expression to *do a yucky*, or to make a poop, therefore became to *do a lucky*. Other cultures would find it strange that we considered ourselves lucky to have done a poop, spawning anthropological theories about my family as constipated or otherwise deviant.

Cultures develop certain etiquette, like answering the phone *hello* or shutting the door when you go to the bathroom, which incidentally was not one of ours. Actually, our bathroom seemed to have its own set of behavioral norms. Using the bathroom for more than two minutes always elicited a yell from downstairs, *Are you alright in there?* This expression served both as a show of concern and a warning not to monopolize one of the most sought after rooms in the house. The question *Is the bathroom available?* eventually broke down into more specific questions like *Is the sink available? Are you using the toilet?* or *Is someone in the shower?* With six people getting ready to leave the house in the morning, the shower became the most significant element of the bathroom, and was expected to be in constant use. Too much down time between showers would result in a panic, and emergency shouts of *The shower is available!* would echo through the house like a security alarm.

My mother even had her own bathroom customs, like not shutting the door or turning on the light when she went to the bathroom at night. "Don't you want the light on?" we'd ask. Like the pre-written dialogue of a religious ceremony, she always answered with the same line: "I know where my bum is."

Many of our codes of conduct were easily understood. Nobody was allowed to swig from the bottle, as in drinking directly from a gallon jug of milk, unless they were finishing off the bottle. Rotten meat was saved for casseroles and stale bread products were collected for the duck pond. If the dog crapped in the house, you ignore it until someone else came home, and pretend that they found it first -- it was the responsibility of the person who found it to clean it up, based on the larger society's belief in finder's keepers.

Our household's biggest source of confusion and conflict concerned the rules associated with workers, and workers' rights, which we collectively refer to as the chores. A worker in my household was defined as any able body that was not my mom. Our society was governed by two head of households. My dad, who was an obvious figure head, held a position of power in name only. My mom, the military backbone, provided the bulk of the political structure and philosophy. Like most sophisticated cultures, or any good organized religion, our charter was full of confusing dictates and contradictory expectations. The chores: my mom always started to delegate the chores with the question *Who's looking for jobs?* It was a system based on the false pretense of individual thought, which my dad was quick to point out. Often the chores were given out as a series of short, confusing dialogues. They usually started out with one of my mom's trick questions, like *Do you think this goes here?* or *How are you at doing the dishes?*

These would be followed up by such contradictory commands as *Think before you act,* and *Don't think just do.*

Our training would culminate in emergency clean-up drills that took place in the waning hours before company arrived, usually an odd assortment of extended family that wasn't overly concerned with the appearance of our house. Here's a sample of how my mom would direct the family unit to prepare for some company:

My mom called the troops into the kitchen. "Pat, Julie, Michelle, Ray – three and four." My brother was Raymond Carey IV, so this meant both him and my dad. Instead of Ray and Ray Jr., my mom often referred to them simply as Three and Four.

"Coming," we all shouted and headed to role call.

"Alright, we have company coming over in under two hours, and there's a lot to do. The living room is full of crap, so we need to get it all upstairs. And I want the upstairs doors open, and none of the crap visible." This was always a tough job, because we needed to fit all the excess stuff in the tiny bedrooms, and somehow keep it out of sight. We had to maximize our use of small areas behind the bed and the L shaped edge of my sisters' room that couldn't be seen from the hallway. Why my mom was so adverse to closed doors upstairs we still have no idea. "Who's lookin for jobs?"

The correct response was of course all of us. We had learned from experience that volunteering for jobs provided us with better chores. "I'll switch the laundry," I said.

"Pat, gather the dirty clothes and then fold the clean laundry when it comes up." She knew I was headed to the cellar because the ice cream was kept down there. A history of half gallons of ice cream full of little finger marks told the story of the laundry chore, but my mom knew she had to tolerate a certain level of rebel activity to avoid an uprising.

"I'll vacuum," Ray volunteered. He had found a way to enjoy vacuuming, claiming that he could match the exact sound that the vacuum made. He would moan and howl long and deep, trying to match the exact pitch of the vacuum. Ray claimed that he could double the volume of noise that he and the vacuum were making by achieving the same pitch.

"Alright, Ray vacuum the whole downstairs and then check with me. And try to keep the howling down. Michelle and Julie, why don't you start on the bedrooms, and let's try to keep everything out of sight." She turned to my dad. "Just stick close by me, I have a lot of special jobs lined up for you."

I finished the laundry and headed to the kitchen to let my mom know I was looking for jobs. My fingers were still cold from the ice cream. All of us would sneak fingers of ice cream, including my dad. But rarely did anyone try to smuggle a spoon. It was like not loading your gun for a robbery, to lesson the charges. If caught, we could plead down to a crime of passion, where the presence of a spoon showed intent, which carried a heavier penalty. "Who's looking for jobs?" The call came from up in the bathroom. I headed upstairs and my mom was staring down into the clothes hamper with a look of despair.

"Do you think this goes here?" She pointed to dirty clothes that were at the bottom of the dirty clothes hamper.

I took a guess, fifty-fifty shot. "Yes."

"No." For some reason my mom generally did not want to use the hamper as a hamper. Clothes were put downstairs in a laundry basket and then sent to the cellar so that someone could finger the ice cream. Maybe it was part of our let's pretend nobody lives here clean up ritual, empty looking bedrooms with no sign of dirty clothes.

"You really think we put dirty clothes in here?" My mom was solidifying her platform of no more dirty clothes in clothes hampers.

I wondered what other plans she might have for the hamper. Maybe a small bedroom for a new sibling. "I just threw them in there because –"

"Think before you act." This was one of my mom's mantras.

"But I thought –"

"Don't think, just do." That was the other of my mom's mantras. "Get this laundry out of here." She stared down into the laundry hamper like she had found our dirty underwear in the garbage disposal. "And then head down to the kitchen, I'll be there in a minute."

I walked by Ray who was vacuuming the same spot over and over again, moaning along in a deep, chanting Ooommmm, hooommmm. I think he had found his Hoover chakra. I headed to the kitchen, looked over my shoulder, and began to chug a gallon container of milk. My mom snuck up behind me, "I hope you're gonna finish that." I breathed in through my nose and polished off almost a half gallon of milk. I staggered over to the trash, bloated with milk – my mom nodded in approval.

"Ray, quit moaning and get in here!" My mom got Ray and me together to coordinate the kitchen chores. "Alright Ray, how are you at doing the dishes?"

Ray didn't like the dishes chore, it didn't have any real melody like the vacuuming. "Not too good."

"Well, then you need the practice. You can wash." She turned to me. "How are you at drying and putting away?"

I was hoping for the trash chore to get another swipe at the ice cream. I had found a broken plastic spoon in the kitchen; it was hidden in my sock awaiting the next cellar chore or prison fight. I tried to play along. "Oh, I'm the best at drying dishes, I don't need any practice."

"Great, if you're the best we'd love to see your work. Here's a towel. Wait, where's your father? Ray. Three!"

"I'm in the bathroom!" My dad yelled from upstairs.

"Are you alright in there?"

"Yeah . . . just going to the bathroom! I feel a little sick."

"Did ya *get* sick?"

"No!"

"Well, let me know when you're looking for jobs!"

"Yes, dear."

I whispered to Ray, "Poor guy is just trying to do a lucky."

Don't flush

Growing up we probably went to the doctor less often than most kids. We went to my mom with all of our ailments. The most common diagnosis was you're fine, pronounced *youah fine*. We would line up and ask my mom medical questions. *Mom, this itches*; diagnosis: don't scratch it, youah fine. *Mom, I have a headache*; diagnosis: kids don't get headaches, when you turn 18 you can have a headache, youah fine. *Mom, I'm sick*. This was always followed with the question, Did you *get* sick? And then usually: no, youah fine.

But I guess what was more unusual about my mom, was the checking of poops. My mom knew of ways to look at your poops and tell if you were sick. I think she could've worked for the FBI as a tracker: *You say we're lookin for a convict. Well I can tell you that whoever made this right here, is definitely not getting their vegetables.* So any time we made unusual bowel movements, we would yell out to her, *Mom, come check my poops*: *mom my poops are green, mom my poops are weird shapes, mom my poops are just one giant poop*. She would call out from downstairs, excitedly, *Don't flush, I'll be up in a minute to see them*. I feel even today I still take a more keen interest than most people in the oddities of my own bowel movements, and whenever I have a particularly strange one, though she's so far away, I long to call out to her, *mom, come check my poops.*

My dad would say, *That's nice talk. Talking about your mother looking at poops. There ya go, this family has an anal fixation.* My dad is always saying that. *This family has an anal fixation; you guys are anally fixated. I really think the whole family has a butt fetish.*

He might have a point. Sure, every family enjoys a little potty humor; but maybe the public farting in my house was a little extreme. For instance when someone farted and the blame was being passed around, if anyone tried to blame my mom she always said the same thing: *If I farted you'd know it.* It was a bold, and irrefutable statement – such power. It was like her platform for political office. *And ladies and gentleman, I promise you, if I farted, you'd know it.*

Last summer I was at my parents' house, and my brother and his pregnant wife were there. They were talking about options for delivering the baby -- home delivery, midwives, nice family kind of talk. Sometimes in a conversation people make a connection in their mind that seems to them like a logical jump from the conversation, but it's hard to see exactly how they got there. Somehow my Dad makes a connection in his mind and decides he has something to add to the conversation. He's been a high school teacher for about twenty five years. He raises his hand from across the room. I look over and well, I call on him, "Yes dad, did you want to add something?"

He sits up. "I just got my first enema the other day." He proceeds to tell us some of the details.

I respond, "Look, I'm not going to call on you anymore if these are the kind of things you want to say."

My dad continues, " . . . and since then my bowel movements have been a little easier, a little different."

My mom perks up, real excited. "Oh honey, I should take a look at those."

Poops come out

I went to my girlfriend's cousin's house for the weekend, in a little town in rural Pennsylvania. They have three little boys – a two year old, a four year old and a six year old. They don't have a shower, only a bath, and the bathroom door has no lock on it. I start the bath, shut the door and take off my shirt. The two year old comes barging through, naked except pointy black cowboy boots. "Booboo." He points to my nipple.

"Yeah, that's my booboo."

He gets a little more emphatic and stomps his tiny boots. "Booboo, booboo." It's kind of a hippie household, where the kids run around naked a little, and their mom breast feeds them to a later age then some. So this two year old is one of those walking, talking infants that walks right up and asks for the boob like he's ordering from the bar. I realize as he gets impatient that he wants me to breast feed him. It would be a much more freaky scene if he wasn't two. If he was, say, 42. Getting screamed at in the bathroom by a naked cowboy, who is convinced that I'm lactating. I try to tell him there's no milk, that no food comes from hairy booboos. I can't really convince him that my booboo has no milk, but I send him downstairs to see his mom.

I shut the door, get undressed and settle into the bath. The door swings wide again, this time the six year old comes in and walks right over to the tub. "I can see your peepee."

Hmmm, I glance down at my peepee beneath the water. "Yup."

He drops his arms down by his side. His body stiffens and he raises his chin, ready for some kind of announcement. Louder this time, "I can see your peepee."

I try to change the subject. "Yeah, what's goin on downstairs?"

"I'm making a drawing."

"Of what?"

"A dragon. It's for you."

"Awe, thanks buddy. Why don't you go finish it and I'll be down in a minute to see it."

"O.K." He turns to head out then pauses, shuffles side to side with some little dance moves, saying: "Peepee, peepee, peepee."

"Alright great, I'll see you later." He leaves the door open and hustles off downstairs. I soap up a little then sink into the tub. I consider getting up for the door, but the water is already getting cold. I close my eyes for a bit.

"Hi Pat." The four year old. He walks in, pulls his pants down, and hops backward onto the toilet seat. He's sitting, smiling from his seat at the end of the tub. I see his feet dangling above the floor. He looks forward and wrinkles his face like fake anger. He grunts, "Come out. Poops come out." His voice grows more throaty, a deep old man's frustration: "Poops, come out. Out." He hops off the toilet like he's leaping from a moving swing. Pants still holding his ankles together, he makes tiny steps over to the tub and leans his face inches from mine. "They won't come out." He looks so serious. I try not to laugh. "The poops won't come out."

I laugh. "Why don't you go try a little more."

He shuffles back, hops up, and with a few more deep

"Poops come out" chants he looks back with a big smile. "They came out."

The reluctant poops are conquered, and I have a moment to rest in the bath before it gets real cold. "I need someone to wipe me." He stands holding his shirt above his belly, smiling.

I offer him a little encouragement. It's good to teach him to fend for himself. "You can do it, go ahead."

He leans over and wipes the poops, well really smears them mostly. He turns and smiles, "How's that?" Each of his cheeks has a thick stripe of tan like a reverse tan line.

I get out of the tub to lend a wiping hand. Immediately he bends over and grasps his ankles like a Russian gymnast. Maybe he's been to yoga class or had a full body cavity search in prison. You can always spot a kid who has gotten his butt wiped before because he gets right in that severe position. And, to be honest, it does make the job a little easier. "Thanks Pat," he says.

We wash our hands together and I feel the tub water. Still a little warm. I take off my towel and get one leg in.

"Booboo, booboo." The two year old peeks around the door.

Then he is run over by his excited oldest brother. "Ahah, I can see your Peepee."

No doors

My bowels scream to be released. Arguments erupt like British Parliament and tickle my insides. I stumble on in search of relief.

As the minutes pass, the number of public toilet seats I'm willing to squat on slowly increases. I visualize the exact line that I'm still not willing to cross; it's not a pretty picture. I round the corner of a large, brick building. Built into a hill, the cavernous belly of the cellar boasts a wooden door with the welcoming logo MEN. Urinals on the right, I spin and pause briefly for the exciting choice of stalls. A drum roll whirls in my head like some disgusting game show where each contestant gets a pint of Ex-lax and a roadmap to the public stalls and fast food chains. Will contestant number two be able to shit in Burger King without buying a value meal? Stay tuned.

I choose the middle stall for its natural sunlight and minimal use, then clean it vigorously and squat. The marble seat stings cold against my cheeks. It's actually a fancy can once you duck inside the splintered doorway. That's the outside door I'm referring to. For some reason, none of the stalls have doors, or even a hint that they were ever meant to. No hinges, holes, or loose fixtures. The stalls are walls of marble muscle, thick and decorative -- makes you feel they had enough cash to finish the job but chose not to. I have a few minutes to myself, a king on his marble throne smirks back at me through a cracked mirror over the sink.

A raspy grumbling announces the arrival of a few old fellows. They're not talking to each other, but a virtual orchestra of bodily sounds backs their entrance into the grand bathroom. Black lung coughs, gasping for air, the booming echo of a dry heave, a waning line of distinction between flatulence and excretion – this is the song of the decay of the human body.

The narrow stall keeps my eyes pointed forward like a horse with blinders. Saggy sweatpants shuffle to a urinal. The wrinkled head bobs neckless from a high sweatshirt to the tune of a walkman. He pauses to savor a beat and then drops the small walkman into a back pocket; the sweatpants sag a few inches past candy striped boxers and the bobbing slows to concentrate on the task. A couple men approach the wall, identify an opening and then leave without consequence. The candy striper takes his time and turns in synch with the big red face next to him. They move toward me with one motion like a step show, then the smaller one drops into a slouch and shuffles off the stage.

The big red face approaches, shoulders and body dangling behind. Intense eyes investigate my situation through thick windshield glasses. He doesn't look away, or make an awkward smirk. He just stares, tilting his head back and forth like a chimpanzee. I return his empty gaze, a poker face.

A crackling echoes from the corners of the room, and music forces its way through ancient speakers. The sound clears. It's Jimmy Durante singing "As Time Goes By." Durante throws his raspy chords around the room, and the big red chimp is still thoroughly perusing my stall. It's quite an intimate stare for such a private occasion. But he doesn't seem aroused or enthused, just like he's old enough that he doesn't need to look away. His age moves him beyond the realm of appropriate behavior. He seems intrigued by my lack of privacy, and suddenly I begin to feel like the chimp. My every bowel movement is studied behind clear glass as scientists and tourists share a fascination with showcasing my private rituals. I begin to wonder if he has any snacks for me. Old men often carry snacks, it's one of the gimmicks of the old man.

"Hey, no doors." His deep voice brings me back to the public stall, squatting in front of an old man. A long shit hangs defiantly from my ass. I try to squeeze my cheeks without showing him the tension in my face. No luck. I sway gently hoping to swing it free, this time trying to keep my upper body stiff. My eyes locked on his, the shit swings and breaks, and a little water wets my ass. I wonder if he's aware of my every movement. I consider telling him to fuck off, but something between competition and camaraderie keeps me silently responding with my eyes. I want to seem totally unaffected, glancing from down the bar instead of with my pants around my ankles and my ass wet. It's as if I'm pretending that I'm not actually taking a shit, just hanging out enjoying the room. I remember that he talked to me. He remains silent now, just nodding his head with a slight frown. "Yeah . . . no doors," I reply after what feels like minutes.

"See ya later." The left side of his lower lip crawls into a smirk and he walks away toward the sinks. I hear myself mutter a few different words of goodbye but nothing comes out. I stare after him like a deceased relative, then spend a few minutes just relaxing on the can. Walking toward the door a stench like dead animals floats up from the trash can. Last night gurgles and burns up my throat, leaving a similar taste. This place is really a shithole. I glance at my watch trying to figure out how long I've been in this bathroom. My best guess is around twenty minutes, but five or forty-five both seem possible.

Stepping into a wall of pale heat, the light spins me a minute before I can focus. The sunshine burns clarity into my mind. The old man bobs his chimp head right into my face and then through the back of my head and onward. I lean back against the brick building.

Pounahgrafee

My mom always wanted us involved in activities, so we wouldn't be hanging around with the bad kids. I lived in a little town about forty-five minutes from Boston. The bad kids in my town hung out downtown, outside the YMCA. They were in a gang that called themselves the Scallions. In case you're not sure what a scallion is, it's basically like a chive, a long thin vegetable with the subtle flavor of a boiled onion. Needless to say, they were fucking badasses.

To keep us away from this kind of trouble, my mom wanted everyone to have a lot of activities. My sisters, my brother and I each had a photocopy of a weekly planner up on the refrigerator. My brother did swimming and boyscouts, one sister was a gymnast, the other a dancer. Each had a schedule with all of their activities on it. Some of the activities went on every day, like my brother's swimming -- SWIMMING was written on Monday with an arrow drawn across the week. My schedule was almost empty. Down the bottom under Monday was written LOOK FOR ACTIVITIES, with an arrow drawn across.

It wasn't like I was a bad kid, I just had the most room in my schedule for getting into trouble -- like the time I got caught with pornos. I had gotten one porn magazine from a kid in middle school, who had some connection with a girl at a convenience store that was willing to sell to him. She was some nineteen year old girl with pimples and braces, but to us she was a whole lot more than that. She was a powerful porn pusher, the head of the South American cartel that dealt magazines to our little middle school porn ring. Five bucks was a tall order. I remember my buddy gave me one ripped out page for free to get me by and encourage some business. One side had a picture of a naked cowgirl, naked except a cute cowgirl hat and a belt she had her thumbs tucked into. I remember thinking she would have looked silly without her belt on, with nowhere to put her thumbs. On the other side was a girl outside in her raincoat – let's just say she was not properly covered up against the elements. I kept it crumpled in pockets and secret hiding places until I saved up enough for my own magazine.

Finally I got my very own dirty magazine. It was a thick one, special edition, *Girls in Lingerie*. All of the poses were of girls doing everyday activities like washing dishes and playing croquet, except they were in their underwear. And they were all looking up with the same expression on their face, like you walked in on them, but they're glad you did. *Oh, I was just playing a little croquet in my underpants, but I'm glad you walked in.*

Enjoyable? Sure. But after a few weeks I was looking for something else. I was twelve years old, a man of the 80s. And the appeal of porn is really in the variety. When a guy seeks out strange, exotic porn -- like *Employees of the DMV Gone Wild* -- he dreams of the days as a little kid when he could get off to pictures of other people's moms in the underwear section of the Kmart catalog.

I found out that my neighbor Tony had a porno also. We looked over each other's merchandise and made the switch. A couple weeks later when my mom was getting in the car to take my sisters to dance class and gymnastics, my neighbor's mom came marching across the street with her son. I could hear my mom outside repeatedly saying the word pornography, and I knew something was up – that's not what they usually talked about. Tony had undermined all that is decent and honorable in any porn ring and given me up to his mom. First rule of a porn ring: don't talk about the porn ring.

My mom was out in the driveway defending me and I was called outside. My mom kept saying the word pornography in a long, drawn out Boston accent. "Pounagrafee. My son is not involved with your son and his pounagrafee."

I backed her up with a complete denial, staring down my rat of a neighbor, as my mom kept assaulting his mom with her repeated long form of the word pornography. I shook my head sadly at the perversity of youth. And then Tony spoke up, "I know where he keeps it, under the bed."

My mom led a four person parade into my bedroom, stuck one foot on the edge of the bed and forcefully turned the mattress against the wall. We all stared down at the metal springs like the opening of an Egyptian tomb. Nothing. Always one step ahead of the game, I had recently moved them to a new spot. We declared my innocence and scoffed at the depravity of other people outside the family.

Halfway down the hall, Tony perked up again, "Oh yeah, sometimes he keeps it in his stack of pants."

My mom stuck her hand in a pile of skinny corduroys and came out holding a dirty magazine. Betrayed by my own corduroys. A couple minutes later I too was in a car that was headed out to dance class and gymnastics.

"You obviously can't be trusted at home alone. You spend all day looking at your Pornography. Pou-nah-gra-fee. Pouah-naaah-graa-fee." She stretched the word all around itself like some kind of contortionist porn, where the face and the tits and the ass all curl around each other into one perverse little package. "That's what you do all day, instead of an activity. Look at pounahgrafee."

I suddenly visualized my empty weekly planner on the refrigerator -- written in block letters on Monday it said LOOK AT SMUT, with an arrow drawn across.

When my dad got home, my parents teamed up for an interrogation. They took turns playing bad cop, bad cop. My mom started prying for names like a McCarthy hearing. But I wasn't about to give up any of my commie porno friends. (That's a little history reference for my dad who says that I'm an academic shell with no sense of history.) Finally I confessed to getting the porn from a friend at school. Now my mom turned her attention to the school. "That's what they do at that school, hand out pornos to kids."

My dad looked up in shock. "They do what?"

My mom just shook her head, "Well, I don't know *what* they do?" She continued with an indictment against the entire American school system.

My Dad took a more personal approach. Pulling a chair in close to me, he began to fire short questions at me in some sort of strange Socratic method. "You like that kind of stuff? Is that the kind of filth you want to bring into my house?"

Then he forced me to get up and bring the porno back to my seat. They had kept it around apparently for, well, evidence or something. I took it out of a wrinkled paper bag that had been added for modesty, the way you cover school books or bottles of booze. He asked me to open it up and take a look at the pages in front of me. This didn't seem so bad. I opened the magazine to a nice picture of a girl ready to play softball. She had all the basic supplies - bat, glove, helmet - except she was naked.

"You like that?" he asked me. I thought of those Co-ed Naked Softball shirts people wear. "Oh you think this is funny? Is this what you want to look at? Do you like that sort of thing?"

I'm telling myself over and over not to respond.

"Well? Is this what you want to do with your time? Do you like that?"

Don't say anything. Just keep your mouth shut.

"Do you like what you see there? You like that?"

Finally I can't take it any more -- I pick my head up and smile, "Well, she's a redhead, not really my type, and lately I've really been into bondage chicks, but the middle school selection is a bit limited."

Massage

On my birthday, my girlfriend took me to a traditional Japanese spa, for their nontraditional coed Wednesdays. Typically, the spa has unisex days, filled mostly with older naked Japanese men quietly relaxing among the hot pools and sauna. This was a day set aside for eastern-minded white folks. A few locals sneak in for a soak or a massage, but mostly Wednesday was dominated by European couples. It was probably listed on a flier at the local hostile as Xtreme hot spring. French boys raced each other across the meditative hot pool. Skinny eurotravelers in brightly striped speedos and backpacks were bungee jumping into the cold plunge. The sign that read *no talking, meditative space* had been taped over with a schedule of activities, most likely by the long-haired youth leader that wore his birkenstocks into the showers. I was called off for my massage just before the chicken fights were scheduled to begin in the steam room.

I was escorted down a hallway of curtains, through a series of cubicles draped with long sheets. A tall thin Rolph pointed, smiled and winked me into a small room and told me to undress. I had already been entertaining myself with a game of Gay or European out in the spa. The game is based on the insight that gay guys and European guys share many of the same fashions and affectations. Let's say, for instance, you come across a long, slender guy squeezing into tight black jeans and a ribbed sweater with flecks of silver in it. Right away you'll be thinking, he's probably gay . . . or European. Extra tight T-shirts, jeans that have Wrangler type patterns on the back, a fading line between sneakers and shoes. These are all fashion traits of gays and Europeans. And as I was smiled at and asked to undress by Rolph, who wore a tight black T-shirt tucked into fitted slacks and some fancy brown sneakers, it became quite obvious to me that he was gay, or at least European.

I lay naked under a sewn together sheet concoction, used only at spas and youth hostels, a sort of perverted bastard child of the bed sheet and the sleeping bag. He told me to go ahead and put my face into that catcher's mask at the end of the massage table, and to let him know how the pressure was, if it was too hard or too soft. I wondered whether I was signed up for the swedish or shiatsu massage, and tried to remember what those words meant. In a moment I realized that regardless of what type of massage this was called, what it meant was pain. Rolph had asked me if I had any particular spots I needed worked on and I told him I didn't. Apparently, he was going to make sure that I had something to tell the next masseuse, as he dug deeper into my shoulder blade looking for, or creating a problem area.

Two thumbs pressed deep into the back of my neck until I felt they were wrestling in my throat, and I wondered if I might have offended Rolph during our brief interaction. My face pressed harder into the leathery ring and then he pushed against my head as if trying to fit it through. My eyes were squeezed open and I saw pasty, hair-covered toes in the brown oval picture frame that I had been shoved into. He had tossed aside the euro-sneaker-shoes for my viewing pleasure. The long feet rolled back onto their heels and then rocked high onto the hairy toes. Uh oh. Owe ah owe. He had used all his weight to dig deep into my lower back, and then left for a moment. Now I opened my eyes to see him standing on a towel. I saw hairy toes curling again. Owe Uh Damn that hurts. Muther. This time he was gone longer. I stared at the oval tan carpet, fearing a scraping sound that was headed toward me. I moved my cheeks a little to feel the warm leather sticking against them, concerned that my face would stay stuck in the oval ring if I tried to escape. I would have to reach down and yank it from the table, hopping through the curtain hallways with my ass hanging out of the white sheet sleeping bag, wearing a catcher's mask. Suddenly the bottom of a chair filled up my view. What was he using the chair – Hey Bastard Ahhh. I screamed to myself without letting on to Rolph, Arrrggghhh -- the yell of a silent pirate subjected to naked torture. Arrrggghhh. Ye nasty gay European mother fucker. I'll get yea back for this.

Rolph now had the elevation to rip me apart. He hopped off of the stool and I waited in agony for the next weapon of choice. Perhaps he was going for a rolling pin to tenderize my back, or a table saw to loosen my tendons. He put on a somewhat soothing tape that sounded like little kids breaking glass bottles on each other's heads and then whispering. I heard that strange suction sound of someone loading their hands up with oil and then the top of my sleeping bag was ripped aside. Enough with the violent rage, Rolph was going to show me his tender side, as he apparently stared down at mine.

I was quickly covered in a thick grease which was rubbed through my hair and in between my toes. Again, I hadn't suggested any particular area to focus on, but he seemed to have chosen my butt and upper thigh. Now it's been my experience with a professional massage that the butt is usually involved, but never occupies any time all to itself. It gets rubbed, pinched, or karate chopped because it lies at the low end of the back, or just gets approached at the top end of a leg rub. But this was something different, a full twenty minutes of unadulterated, concentrated butt love. Sensual, lubricated massage that started on the butt, and stayed on the butt, with no room for mistake or distinction. And then the occasional ball grazing stroke. Here and there the edge of a rub on the upper thigh would just flick the edge of my balls. I figured Rolph would have noticed the change in texture, as easily as I noticed the seeming sudden change in our relationship. Here was a man who had previously never touched my balls. I began to envision how I would react to this scenario if he were just a guy on the street, or in the sauna at the YMCA. You begin to negotiate, and renegotiate your comfort level as you lay naked, groped by a gay or European man named Rolph. Let's say I was in the supermarket, and a European guy accidentally brushed up against my ass. No big deal, and if I had just spilled a bottle of Crisco oil on myself, I suppose it's possible that his hand might slip and lightly graze my balls. Sure.

When a woman massages me, it's easy for me to close my eyes and engage in a rich fantasy life. Growing up, massage for me was like a move you would put on a girl, an excuse to do something almost sexual that might just get you there. Guys become master masseuses. Oh, the bra doesn't allow me to make my patented full karate chop, you better take it off. So when a guy gets a professional massage from a woman, it's easy to slip into that, oh-that-stripper-really-wants-me mentality. Laying perfectly still, the mind wanders during a sensual massage. Oh yeah, she put her breast against me on purpose. I love the way she keeps grazing my balls.

So this massage apparently was swedish instead of shiatsu, or shiatsu instead of swedish, and instead of a woman gently massaging me with sensual oils, it was a guy covering me with oils and digging deep into my spine. Apparently, whatever massage I received, the term for it basically means having your balls gently nudged in a pool of oil and getting the shit kicked out of you. Kind of like the whole hot pool, cold plunge mentality of the spa. I can see why the Europeans love the Xtreme nature of this eastern stuff, getting tattoos of yin and yang on their shoulder or left butt cheek. The duality of experience, of pain and pleasure, and the duality of Rolph – both gay and European.

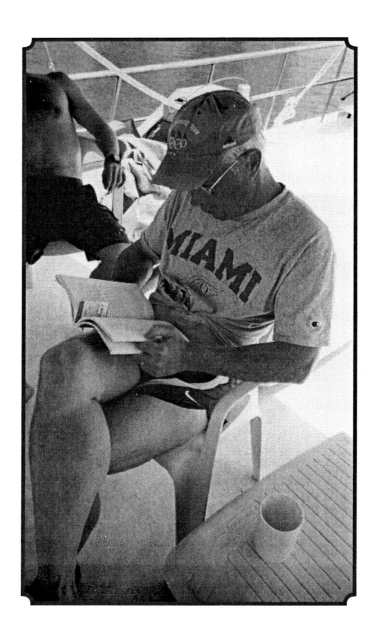

Homersexuals

We're all in our twenties and thirties now, but my dad still treats us like little kids when we're staying at home. He treats everyone like his kids. We'll all be hanging out in the living room up late -- me, my brother and sisters, our partners, assorted friends -- and he'll come down the stairs in a half stupor, wearing nothing but his tighty whities, or loosey whities as we like to call them because they are his own personal take on big girl undies. He comes downstairs to make his announcement: "It's getting very late. You should all go to bed."

And we'll ask him, "Even Gajohnson and Diane," pointing to our friends.

"Yeah, it's late for them to be up too. We have a lot to do tomorrow, and you all need to get on our schedule." He's often worried about our conflicting schedules, especially when people fly home from other time zones. "Kids, go to bed, you need to get on east coast time." Then he stumbles back up stairs, threatening to return again later.

My father is often hilarious, and somehow he never understands why. "What's so funny about what I do? I must be a great guy for you to hang around, because everything I do is *so* hilarious." The late night underwear fashion show is one of our favorites, but my dad has a few other interesting outfits. He's like our own dress up Barbie with special outfits for different occasions. Night Time dad is a favorite, but there's also Beach Wear dad. He has a special little fashion trick where he ties up his shirt just above his belly, usually above some sexy slit up the side track lingerie shorts. He looks like a sporty southern Barbie flirting along the beach. "Oh, I suppose you think this is funny to?" He always thinks it isn't funny because he has a logical explanation for it. "I know you think this is hysterical but my shorts are wet and I want to keep my shirt dry."

We'll tell him, "Yeah dad, you're right, walking the beach with you're father dressed as Daisy Duke isn't funny."

He's a track coach so when Beach Time Barbie gets cold, he sports some close-fitting track tights. Striped down the side, tapering down into stirrups. At first he wore them under his pants, then on their own at track practice. Soon they were going everywhere. He tucks in his T-shirt and wears low sneakers so you can see the stirrups that wrap around his ankles. He turns into some kind of Sporting/Super Barbie, man about town in his long slender tights. "Dad, are you going to the supermarket in those tights?"

"Yeah, what's wrong with them?"

"Nothing. You gonna fight some bad guys while you're out? Going to get some milk and eggs and reroute a nuclear bomb, maybe stop in on Lex Luthor?"

"Oh, I suppose you think this is funny. You guys obviously know nothing about track and field. These are track tights. What's so funny about track tights?"

He's always cracking us up but never quite gets what's so funny about it. He's a straight man from a comedy routine. Well, a straight man trapped in a gay man's tights.

My dad strives to be open to other lifestyles, cultures, sexual orientations. Growing up on the eastcoast homosexuals were called queah. *What are you queah?* We grew up among kids constantly calling each other *queah, fag, queah* for everything from backing down from a fight to taking a shower. So my dad would have none of that kind of talk in our house. We used the word gay, and then one day he came home and told us we weren't allowed to say gay anymore – "They are homosexuals" he told us. But since we didn't know any openly gay folks growing up, my dad became the spokesperson for all of the homosexuals. It was like he was coming back from a secret eastcoast meeting and giving us the updates – "They now prefer to be called homosexuals." Or as my dad's Boston accent made it, *homersexuals.* He brought back the *r* that had been so violently ripped from all the *queahs,* and returned it to *homersexuals* to make up for it.

As we grew older, my parents began to have some gay friends. At first they were not very discriminating. Just looking for any guy who sleeps with other men, or what we refer to as a lesbian. Heterosexuals need not apply. My parents befriended this wealthy, eccentric, flamboyant gay dancer. I remember my dad telling me how the homersexual in question went to shake his hand and instead reached down and touched my dad's privates. We asked him, "Dad, what did you do?"

He responded, "Nothing, I just smiled, I'm not homophobic."

These days, my brother and I live in San Francisco, my older sister in LA, and my younger sister lives in Miami. We have all found ourselves living in homersexual meccas. We like to joke about how disappointed my dad is that none of us are gay, but at least we have more gay friends for him, most of whom will shake his hand without reaching for his crotch. Sometimes the excitement of California still impresses my dad, even with his long history of supporting gay pride. My older sister in LA is friends with two gay guys from Mexico that are adopting a kid. So my sister and my dad were going to bookstores looking for a book on gay parenting. My sister would ask people in the store, "Where can I find a Spanish book on queer parenting?"

And my dad kept saying, "Wait till I tell people back home. We're in a bookstore in LA looking for a book on *queer* parenting . . . in Spanish."

But even my dad has his limits. The other day my parents were going to schedule massages for their anniversary. And it turns out that the place they were calling has a blind guy that gives massages. And my dad says, "I don't mean to sound homophobic, but I don't want to get a massage from a blind guy." I guess he figures hey, the guy can't see where he's going, and who knows where he'll end up.

When my sister, my brother and I first moved to California, that really stirred things up at home. We started to throw around words like queer, and we had friends that referred to themselves casually as dykes or fags. We would bring gay friends back to our house in Boston, and my dad would say, "Hey, we don't use that kind of language. I don't care if you are a fag, in this house you're a homersexual."

Eventually he grew into the idea a little. "It's like a take back thing. So then queah is bad, but queer is OK." If people around Boston start taking back their queah, everything will become totally confusing. Now when my dad puts on his winter Barbie tights or ties up his shirt like Daisy Duke, we say, "Dad, you look a little queah." And he looks upset. Then I tell him, "No, you look queer, real queer," with a fist motion of solidarity.

And my dad replies, "Thanks Pat, you're real queer too."

Trainers

Trainers – they provide lessons like driver's education, CPR skills, and workplace safety instructions. They live in the shadows of teachers and coaches; shine a light down the halls of education and you'll see them scurry like rats. Some work full-time as health or safety instructors. They line their classrooms with pictures of dated celebrities enjoying a healthy lifestyle: Kenny Loggins bikes with a safety helmet, Arsenio Hall reads Dr. Seuss, and Melanie Griffith squints at *Grapes of Wrath* through safety goggles. The best posters are faded warnings from celebrities that pre-date their scandals, like public service announcements from Pete Rose, Pee-wee Herman and George Michael.

The real core trainers work part-time or as volunteers, straggling in from strange outside lives for a workshop at the library. They live on the outskirts of every town, and spend their time making vague references to outside clubs and lifestyles, displaying a strange devotion to one skill or organization. I come in contact with them all the time, but never see them outside of their element going to the dentist or buying eggplant. I've been schooled by some of the finest. My instructor for Comedy Traffic School apparently didn't read the brochure, and found a difficult time bringing comedy or traffic into his lectures. The only thing smaller than his rat/ dog were his Richard Simmons striped shorts. He spent three days relating uncomical stories that occasionally touched the subject of traffic. He told us tales about picking up his dog's poop, and performing on cruise lines to unimpressed crowds. Then he would throw in a true false question about the shape of stop signs.

While I worked in the field of social work, we had countless trainings on subjects that had titles like segments on *Mr. Roger's Neighborhood*: *What can we do for ourself today*, or *When a client is angry, they're not angry at me*. A round, bearded biker with a leather vest trained us on HIV prevention. He told us about all the girls that want to ride his *hog* and the risks of contracting HIV. He'd start off, "OK, let's just say there was this friend of mine." Then he winked and nudged his elbow four of five times. "And this so called friend of mine was being hunted down by a busty blonde at a biker rally . . . and I mean busty." Two weeks later we're sitting in the same room for a three hour training about how different colored pens can brighten up a brainstorming exercise. The last two hours after lunch were dedicated to the idea that alternating colors on a piece of paper makes for easier visibility. I declined to attend part two of that training, having already mastered the insight that just because they smell delicious, we still shouldn't eat the Sharpie pens.

I have met strange lifeguard instructors, and bigots that teach multicultural awareness. I was trained by a health inspector that loved to say he was an expert in the FBI, and later explained the term Food Born Illnesses. But if you're just going for consistently weird, you can't really beat the folks from the Red Cross that teach first aid and CPR. They freak out eight year old boyscouts and convince them that rescues are necessary all around them. If you fall down near a YMCA you'll be quickly mummified in toilet paper and responsible for a large ambulance bill. Here's one of my more precious memories of a training on CPR and First Aid:

A long mustache pointed down to his round chest, which was neatly tucked into tiny tan shorts. Skinny hairless legs paced around a swollen barrel chest, like some bird's mating ritual. "C-P-R," he called out the letters in the low, deep howl of a drunk and belligerent Texas cheerleader. I thought if he unbuttoned his shirt, the T-shirt beneath it would read: *I perform the heimlick maneuver, that's what I do.*

He spent most of the day relaying stories, tales of brave rescues and the imminent dangers that surround us. A lollipop was a choking hazard, a walkman a deadly distraction, and a sharp high heel shoe had somehow pierced his cousin's cheek. He had a real taste for emergency response, almost a scary kind of eagerness. I imagined him building tourniquets to stop paper cuts. And giving himself paper cuts as an excuse to build tourniquets.

But mostly he filled the afternoon with stories of everyday objects that had been used as medical tools. "You can look through the Red Cross catalog and you'll find all kinds of beautiful instruments and equipment. These are some gorgeous pieces really." He stopped and ripped a catalog in half. "But out in the streets, in the concrete jungle . . . we don't have that luxury." He continued with his alternate class syllabus, letting us in on "the little things the Red Cross don't want you to know." He seemed particularly excited by the idea of an emergency tracheotomy. He was desperate to shove a hollow pen into somebody's throat.

But he reminded us that the struggles he faced as a "public safety watchdog" -- which I took to mean an unemployed guy who paces the streets with a well sharpened Bic -- were not even close to the severe emergencies and lack of proper equipment that his wife faced in the ER. An older woman asked him where his wife worked, probably afraid to use that hospital in the future. She was excused from the class and thereafter referred to as the Red Cross spy.

Apparently his wife worked in a public hospital in the OB/GYN unit of the ER. He grew more animated, acting out the inadequate conditions she worked under. "One leg has to hold the light stand in place while she balances her body with the other. She'll have one hand on the monitor, and one hand holding the light." He was about to fall over under the strain and difficulty of his mime. "With her other hand she gets in there and checks it all out." We were all disconcerted by his short, stabbing strokes. One woman let out a soft moan as he continued to show us how his wife prodded her patients. What was slightly more disconcerting than his wife stabbing at a patient's crotch, was the image of an emergency ob-gyn with three hands.

Academic shell

The thousands of students my dad has taught can be broken down into three categories: good kids, kiss asses and bullshit artists. He has spent twenty-five years at an all boys high school, as a history teacher and track coach. Conversations with my dad about former students usually start with a name and then one of the categories, as if it were the student's title. "Jimmy Shelton, good kid, wrote a paper on the strange diet of Napoleon," or "Tim Dupa, bullshit artist, thinks I don't know a copied paper when I see one." Our favorite category, sort of a level of prestige within one of the categories, is the colossal bullshit artist. My dad reserves this title for those students that have really distinguished themselves above and beyond the typical bullshit, a sort of magnum cum laude distinction in bullshit. These are the kinds of students that put the artist in bullshit artist. "Joe Davenport, colossal bullshit artist, tells me he can't take a test because he has a brutal rash creeping up his thigh. So I said, show me."

"But dad, wasn't that the kid that turned out to have scabies and they sent him home for a couple weeks?"

"Yeah, but that's not my only example, trust me, colossal bullshit artist."

On a rare occasion someone comes along that warrants a category completely to themselves. One track kid actually walked in front of a javelin and got pierced in the shoulder -

- he became the neanderthal. "Rob Peterson, the neanderthal, didn't bring his uniform to school so he ran the mile in a button down shirt." After years of exhibiting a general lack of historical knowledge, I too earned my very own distinction, the academic shell. "You're an academic shell," my dad would tell me. "People think you know things. You do well in school, somehow you squeak by and get good grades in history without having any real sense of history. An academic shell, the appearance of knowledge."

My general knowledge of say world politics, or American history, is pretty poor. But if you hit on the right niche my knowledge of history can be extensive. I grew up in a small town on the east coast, where the Spirit of '76 painting is hung in the town hall. Come on academic shells, you know the big picture with the white-haired guy that looks like Jim from Taxi playing the flute, marching with the little drummer boy. We lived just miles from Salem, Massachusetts, of the witch trial fame. So growing up in school our history teachers focused intensely on the local history. What we learned most about were the witch trials and the whaling industry. Any kid I went to middle school with might have a vague sense of Lewis and Clark, like, "Oh yeah, the guys that wanted to hook it up with Sacajawea." They might have a general idea that the history of the United States is full of wars or at least heated arguments. But ask any fellow student of mine about how they tortured witches or different types of whaling harpoons and you'd think they were local tour guides. We may think that NAFTA is a company that makes vanilla wafers, but it's common knowledge in my town that witches were convicted with spectral evidence, a type of evidence based on the witnessed activities of a person's spirit. As for the whaling industry, not only do we know that pictures carved in whale bone are called scrimshaw, but we made replicas of them in class.

I had one history teacher in middle school that focused primarily on the whaling industry, and he seemed to have a solid grasp on the concept of the academic shell. His role was to create assignments and busy work for us that appeared to be academic, but carried with them no real learning. Mr. Orlen was a long standing pillar of the middle school, known widely for his intolerance in the classroom and his willingness to fail students. Succeeding in his class was less a matter of knowledge and insight, and more an issue of menial labor. He would burden us with countless hand outs, requiring every page to be labeled with our name, student number, and address. Also, every page had to be three-hole punched, and each hole covered on both sides with those little useless life-saver stickers so that none of the pages would wander off. As a fellow history teacher, my dad was quick to let us know that Mr. Orlen was ridiculous, just based on the assignments I came home with. After the first parent teachers night, my dad added that Mr. Orlen was also a colossal bullshit artist.

Late in the school year, the heat crept in the windows with the promise of summer. We had already filled several three ring binders with strange handouts on the whaling industry. Mr. Orlen had exhausted the more legitimate historical sources in the first twenty pounds of handouts. We now spent tedious hours placing stickers on articles about whaling boat toilet designs and seamen's etiquette. The class dragged heavy bags filled with photocopies of whaling tattoos and lists of the top ten things to do with whale fat. The sun pushed it's way through the blinds, unusually hot for May weather. The school had created a new dress code rule earlier that year. Students had to wait until June 1st to wear shorts to school. The new rule hadn't been given much attention until the summer seemed to be ahead of schedule, and Sally strolled into Mr. Orlen's class wearing a short pair of jean shorts.

Not one for bending the rules, Mr. Orlen quickly dismissed her to the office. Pleading that none of her other teachers had cared only inspired his discipline. As Sally left, the boys began to defend her right to wear short shorts; a sudden and unusual interest in social justice and freedom of expression grew among the boys. Mr. Orlen sedated the room with detailed slides of men in hip boots wading in fields of whale blubber.

By the end of school, I had gathered a dedicated crowd of twenty-six boys ready to wear shorts the next day, just as Sally had. Well, not the short jean shorts, some of us didn't really have the legs for that. The next day came with rumors of Sally getting suspended from school, and a handful of us showed some leg in her defense. Only seven of us pulled through, well eight, if you count one guy that wore really short pants because he got nervous but still wanted to help. Seven was enough to keep us from individually being sent to the office, and we were told that Sally's situation was still being considered. The strong seven spread the word like disciples of Sally and her short jean shorts. I paraded my skinny, hairless legs around campus, drumming up support for a full-scale leg showing the next day.

The following day found over one hundred middle schoolers sporting everything from tan shorts to flowery bathing suits, from butt-huggers to nut-huggers. About one hundred students and one faculty member revealed their legs that day. The one pair of knees we really hadn't expected or wanted to see was Mr. Orlen's. As we laughed into history class, excited by our newfound short-pants politics, Mr. Orlen looked unusually amused. His top was the normal British Professor kind of look he usually went for, a shirt and tie tucked into a sweater vest. His shoes were the usual brown loafers. Really, it was the middle section that was the most troubling. He looked like one of those books of animals or people where you can flip a third of the page at a time, creating an old lady with a beer gut and duck's feet. The middle section matched, but looked quite odd. He had tan shorts that came just above his knees. The strange part was his argyle socks that stretched from his loafers to his knees, like fancy patterned knee-high stockings. It gave him the appearance of someone not in shorts, but rather caught in their underwear. Kids began to ask him questions, make jokes, and holler at the strange sight of his bare knees and high socks. He just leaned back and smiled, as if the verbal abuse was a perfect part of his planned lecture for the day.

Mr. Orlen smiled, "It's distracting, isn't it? Much like Sally's shorts before the first day of June."

His point was lost on us. One of the boys relayed what many of us were thinking, "No offense man, but seeing your knees is nothing like Sally in those jean shorts."

Mr. Orlen invited discussion about his unusual attire, then spent ten minutes talking about the dress code. "Ahah, do you see how much class time we've wasted already, just because I showed up in shorts today. Truly it is a distraction. Look, everyone is whispering and making comments about it, and we can't move on to the day's discussion of whale teeth used as jewelry, and why the practice is no longer popular today."

I raised my hand for a rare contribution in history class. "Ah, Mr. Orlen. I don't think it's the fact that you're wearing shorts that is so distracting."

"Interesting, I'd love to hear this." Mr. Orlen licked his lips at the possibility of intelligent discourse on the subject.

I continued, "I think it might be your combination of shorts and loafers, or maybe because you look like an idiot, with your socks pulled up so high."

I wondered how my dad would react, knowing he would be getting a call about this later that night. With this comment I had taken myself out of the typical student categories of good kid and kiss ass. Perhaps he would consider me a colossal bullshit artist. But faced with a colossal bullshit artist as a teacher, maybe I was a revolutionary like one of those early guys that hated the British so much, defiant in the face of an oddly dressed tyrant. I'd use a reference here, but in addition to my possible status as a bullshit artist or a revolutionary, at my core I am forever an academic shell.

Witch Museum

My parents' house overlooks Salem Harbor: across the water two lone buildings frame the horizon -- the steeple of our church and the cylindrical towers of the power plant that fed into the harbor where we swam. In between lies the oldest section of Salem, the area well known for the witch trials. It all happened just miles from where I grew up: the hysteria, the trials, and the witch hangings.

I may be shamed by European backpackers' knowledge of world history, but my historical grasp of the Salem witch trials is downright impressive. In World History we would discuss Europe for a week, and brush through Asia and Africa on a half-day; but we spent months investigating the details of Salem's infamous witches. Our school field trips were to dungeons and gallows, spending most of the time posing for morbid pictures. The local schools are decorated with images of children laughing as they stick their heads and hands through the stockades, or rolling their eyes back and letting their head go limp for a hanging snapshot.

Old town Salem is covered with tourist attractions that promise gruesome history: The Witch Dungeon, The Gallows, and assorted smaller museums. The local shops sell historical texts, witch costumes, and pentagram necklaces. Many of the

shops stretch the definition of witch-related goods, stacking
satanic spell books next to fetish wear and nudie playing cards.
And somehow the theme of witches that has characterized
Salem for decades has suddenly sprouted an interest in pirates.
Pirate museums, shows, dinner theaters and local one-eyed
personalities have nestled alongside the witch attractions and
become quite popular with tourists. *Come to Salem and we'll
hang yer wench for bein a witch. Arrrgggghhh!*

Despite it's convenient location just blocks from my
family's church, old town Salem is not a great place to go
shopping for Baptism gifts. My sister Michelle and I learned
this the hard way when we were chosen as the godparents for
our newborn nephew. Last minute religious icon shopping
can be a tricky task, especially in an area dominated by
witchcraft. All the pendants are crystals and pentagrams, the
stuffed animals are witches and trolls, and the spiritual books
are mostly elaborate essays trying to legitimize pot smoking
as a religious rite. After considering the least frightening troll
doll we could find, and a children's book on the various uses
of hemp, we settled on an Irish claddagh pendant.

Shops and strange personalities litter the cobble stone
streets of Salem, bringing in swarms of summer tourists.
Salem's Gallows attract morbid curiosity while the skeeball
and mini-golf of Salem Willows attracts a more sophisticated
crowd. But one place stands out in my mind and continues
to attract my business – the Salem Witch Museum. Though
most of its visitors are school children and Europeans, I am
part of a small but dedicated crowd of locals that provided
repeat business.

The Witch Museum has more official, sanctioned guides to
their show -- but here is mine:

Welcome to the Salem Witch Museum. Some pimply high
school kid will usher you inside a square, dimly lit room.
Most of the people will begin to sit around the edges of the
room, in uncomfortable wooden bench seating. I recommend

you sit on the floor around the glass circle. As soon as you sit down, others will begin to join you, and hopefully you can win over the standing room only folks.

The room becomes dark and the glass circle glows bright red. A loud booming voice-over fills the room, and you are transformed into the Puritan days of old Salem. Paper mache scenes are illuminated throughout the room, each one a short scene that builds toward the growing hysteria of the witch trials. The scenes provide courtroom dialogue and testimonials from accused witches. The voice-over is backed with gushes of wind and voices of young girls' crying out. A giant paper mache devil hangs over the room with glowing red eyes.

The decrepit faces of paper mache mannequins that have not been well kept provide the most eerie effect. Deformed judges howl at accused witches and concerned spectators watch hangings through melting eyes that rest low on their chins. I won't describe each detail, but the two most important characters in the presentation are clearly Giles Corey and John Proctor. Giles Corey lights up in a prison cell as men are slowly piling rocks on his chest. He refuses to confess to being a witch, to keep his family from losing their property rites. If he confesses, he will be hung and all of his assets will become property of the government. The voice asks, "Giles Corey, are you a witch?" After a pause, a loud murmur becomes a strange moan, which seems to go on for about a minute: "Mmmmmeeeeeeerrrrrrrrrrr.Mmmm mmmmmmooooaaaaaaaaa.Mmmmmmmmmmmmmmmmmmm mmmmmmmmmmmmmmmmmmmmmmmmmmmmmmeeeeeee eeeeeeeeeeeehhhhhhhhhMmmmmmmmmmmmmmmmmmm mmmmmoooooooooooooooooooooooooaaaaaaaaaaaaaaaaaaa Mmmmmmmmmmmmmmeeeeeeeeeeeeeeeeeeeeeeeeeeeeerrrrr rrrrrrrrrrrrrrrrrrrrrrrrr. Finally his response breaks through the slow, incoherent moaning: "More weight." Tragedy fades into comedy as the audience alternates between empathetic gasps and fits of laughter. The recording continues with the sound of boulders hitting Giles Corey's chest and another shorter cry of pain. The crowd giggles. The museum has elevated a truly heartbreaking historical moment to another level, almost a *National Lampoon's Salem Witch Trials.*

Giles Corey is one of the highlights of the show, but the Witch Museum has saved the most brilliant piece of narration for the legendary John Proctor. The light illuminates a statue of John Proctor standing with his dog and a gun. The voice-over deepens, reaching an almost James Earl Jones intensity: "During this dark hour in our nation's history, there were a few heroes that emerged . . . he was even said to have once taken an afflicted girl over his knee, and temporarily spanked the witch out of her."

The recording ends with a warning about persecuting people for their differences. And one last note reminds the audience that the total number of people killed in the Salem witch trials pales in comparison to the witch trials that happened in England. The lights come on and the tourists leave with a profound sense of American history. Those from the states pause for a moment to be shamed by America's past and to be thankful for their American freedoms -- but most importantly they are glad at least that they are not British.

A recent addition to the museum discusses the political ramifications of the Salem witch trials, comparing the events to similar incidents of hysteria turned persecution from around the world. The exhibit also breaks down modern definitions of witches, with interactive exhibits about the traditional image of the witch and information about modern witchcraft. The last time I visited the museum, I saw a little girl pause in front of two statues of practitioners of the Wiccan religion. The exhibit discusses the roots of the Wiccan religion. The girl looked up at her daddy as he was reading the plaque beside them. "Who are they?" she asked him.

Her dad looked down into her big brown eyes. "Those are the freaks from the Renaissance Fair." He read on. "Oh yeah, and they're dope fiends."

The museum continues to provide insight about the persecution of marginalized groups in our society. The lessons stay with us long after the image of rotting mannequins has faded from our minds. But for me, the Salem Witch Museum will always be about the lingering moans of Giles Corey, and of course the brave John Proctor. I would like to hope that under such volatile circumstances, that maybe all of us could have the courage to put our own safety aside, for a moment, and take a young girl over our knee.

My Intanet

I could just say that we were one of the last families in our town to get cable, Atari, and the internet, but that doesn't really tell the whole story. You need to have some idea of the town itself. I grew up in a small town about forty-five minutes north of Boston. That's what I usually tell people when I'm far from home. I'll start by saying I'm from the east coast, or from around Boston. People who consider themselves from the east coast will light up and tell me where they are from. Let me take a moment to clarify the definition of the east coast. For people like myself that grew up around Boston, the east coast goes west to New York, and down to Washington, D.C. I have had my fill of people eagerly telling me they are also from the east coast, only to find out they hail from South Carolina or Ohio. Just because your property butts up against the Atlantic ocean, doesn't make you an east coaster. If you're from one of the states falling between D.C. and Florida, then you're from the south, and nobody really wants to claim Ohio.

Those who are familiar with the Boston area get increasingly excited and want more specifics, except of course Boston natives who generally are not impressed. But the others press on, *yeah I know Boston. Where exactly are you from?* I'll tell people that I'm from Marblehead, though I'd rather let them know that my dad's family is from Revere, where my family sells roast beef sandwiches. Revere is closer to the personality of my family than Marblehead, which conjures up strange images for people who know it. Marblehead is a cute, oceanside town full of history, bed and breakfasts, and wealthy white families. I'll get approached by a guy in Dockers pants and a Ralph Lauren shirt with a white sweater tied around his neck. His wife will be playing with large pearls just above a brooch that resembles a cop's shield. When I tell them I'm from Marblehead they'll immediately feel at ease and tell me that *Marblehead is absolutely fabulous, a lovely little sailing community.* The other response I get is a thick Boston accent saying something like, *youah a wicked snaab, then. Youah family's friggan rich, huh?*

Growing up we never felt part of a sailing community, and anyone who has ever driven past one of my family reunions would have a difficult time calling me a wicked snob. My family owns a house that my parents bought for twenty-five thousand dollars. It was a summer cottage that we spent several years winterizing and turning into a regular house, during which time we lived in it year round. The house overlooks Salem Harbor, the part of the harbor that faces the power plant. We live right by a beautiful beach where we would swim every day in the summer. The harbor has been rated one of the most polluted in the nation, and sometimes after swimming we would spend hours picking strange black dots off of our skin. As for sailing, well one year somebody did give us a sail boat, which blew a hole and sank before we got to use it. We would fish fifty feet offshore, dropping string tied to hooks from our grandfather's rowboat. Until I was about sixteen years old, I thought fishing rods were used only by professional fishermen and in the movies.

My mom was a part-time waitress, and my dad worked as a high school teacher and at the family's roast beef stand. It's not real surprising that we were one of the last families in the town to get new gadgets like cable or a computer. We lived on a tight budget in a town filled with rich people. However, the timing of our introduction to these inventions is not as significant as the effect they had on us. We may have seen something at our friends' houses for ten years, but it arrived at our house like a futuristic product from another planet. Cable finally arrived after almost all of the kids had left the house, and we got Atari from my uncle in response to us begging for a Playstation. But the invention that had the most profound effect on us was the microwave.

After they took center stage in every TV sitcom kitchen, microwaves spread fast throughout the nation. It was as if stoves had suddenly refused to cook, and microwaves were willing to break strike lines. Scabs. Years later when all the excitement had died down, we were still cooking popcorn in a big metal pan on the stove, and mixing leftovers into big glass pans as casseroles. We had seen microwaves all over, and had used them a bit, but always with a little restraint. Someday, we thought, we'll get a microwave of our own and then we'll really see what this little hot box can do. It's like test-driving a Porsche with the dealer in the passenger seat, thinking if you weren't here I'd wrap this thing around a telephone pole real good. My dad arrived home with a box, like the uncle in movies that brings crates back from exotic countries. A pet monkey? Gremlins? Even better, our very own microwave. No time for directions, we set it up on the counter and began gathering things to cook. My aunt Edith had come up the street to see what all the hype was about.

"What's good to cook in a microwave?" we asked her.

She looked around at our pile of food and household items. "Well, I heard eggs are no good, they come out all rubbery."

"Wow," Julie exclaimed. So that was our first ever microwave item. We split an egg and then left one in the shell. Both came out rubbery like fake eggs in a kid's kitchen toy set. The broken egg we ate. *Hey, this is weird. Here you try it. Nasty, you gotta try this.* The whole egg we peeled and bounced around the kitchen, convinced that we had unleashed an unknown power of the microwave. After turning carrots soft and timing ice cream melts, we moved on to the nonperishables, like shoes. Just before Aunt Edith headed out, she warned us to be careful about putting metal in the microwave. We found a plastic bag with a baggy tie on it and made our first little microwave fire. Thanks Edith.

The kind of excitement that young kids bring to new technology never died out at my house. Years after the four of us left the house, my parents continue to find their own drama in emerging technologies. A few years ago my parents finally started to replace the phones that the phone company gave them in the early 70s. They got new phones not because of the crackling sounds and occasional electrical shock to the ear, but because my dad found out that people generally don't pay phone rental charges anymore. They were paying about seven dollars per phone every month, a type of service charge that had been mostly eradicated about twenty years before. Still, they were resistant to the idea of replacing the phones. "So if I go buy a new phone and plug it in at my house," my dad asked in complete sincerity, "How does the phone know to ring at *my* house?"

"What?" I pictured a smiling cartoon phone with my dad's confused face.

"How does the phone know that it's now my phone?"

I tried to find an example for him. "Dad, if you go drive to your sister's house and take her phone, then plug it in here, and someone call's your sister's phone number, do you think it'll ring here?"

He looked upset. "You want me to steal my sister's phone?"

More recently, the emergence of various types of phones has really tripped up my dad. He is convinced that he has a cellular phone. "Oh, just call my cell phone, I got a nice one."

Instead, he actually has a cordless phone which he refuses to leave off the charger for over two minutes. "Yeah, alright, I gotta go. I'll call you back, I gotta charge my cell phone up." Of course, there's also the time that my dad tried to page me by talking into my sister's pager like a walkie talkie.

However, my parents are truly on the cutting edge these days with their use of the internet. When I was in high school, the whole family typed papers on a typewriter, including my parents who were both high school teachers. Around the time most of our friends got Macintoshes, we got a TRS-80. Basically, you could use it for two things – writing papers and playing word games. Our favorite game was psychiatrist. The opening line of the game read, *Welcome to Psychiatrist. What's your problem?* We would spend hours writing responses and engaging the computer in a dialogue. Like any good psychiatrist, the TRS-80 would respond mostly with questions, like *Why are you asking me what's your problem? What is it that makes me this dick?* Or *I do not understand. How do I go fuck yourself?*

My parents currently have a computer made by Hyundai, whose computers are slightly less respected than their cars. When my mom announced that they had finally gotten the internet on a computer she got from school, we all rejoiced. "I got my in-ta-net all set up," she said, dissecting the syllables with a sharp Boston accent. Home all together for Christmas, we wanted to see my parents surf the internet, push the boundaries of their technology, make a rubber egg or a plastic bag fire. We asked my mom if she wanted to check the internet for movie showtimes or see if the forecast predicted snow on Christmas. "Oh, my intanet doesn't have that." Performing a search or checking our email accounts got turned down with the same words, "Yeah, sorry, my intanet doesn't have that either."

It turns out that my mom had a modem, and could access the school's database. In the last few months my parents have upgraded from my mom's intanet to the internet. My dad hates the way that the internet connection cuts out when a call comes in on his cell phone, and is convinced that this would not have been a problem with his old phones. The other day my older sister helped my dad buy a plane ticket online and set up a free email account. He called a day later in a panic. "I don't mean to sound ungrateful, but this email account you set me up with is wicked expensive."

"Dad, it's a free email," she tried to console him.

"Well, I just got charged one hundred ninety dollars for the account. Even if that's for the whole year, that's a little pricey. I don't know about this hotwire email, I should've just stayed with my AOL."

Michelle explained that his new email was a hotmail account, but that he had purchased a plane ticket at hotwire.

"Oh, that's not too bad for flying to California," he said, relieved. "But for an email account it's pretty hefty."

Lately, when people hear I'm from Marblehead and call me a wicked snob, I think of my family bouncing a rubber egg around an unfinished kitchen floor. And if an uppercrust couple seems impressed by my hometown and wants to get in touch with the family, I tell them, "I'd give you an email, but my mom's intanet doesn't have that. You'll have to call my dad on his cell phone."

Little People

My dad stared out the window, as the sun glistened off the water: "I like that guy from *Willow* -- you know that short, little person." He looked back to the ocean like he was part of a more sophisticated conversation. "I don't want to call him the wrong thing, I saw a program on TV the other day. I'm not sure if he's a dwarf -- I can't remember if it was the dwarves, or the midgets, but one of them, something like forty percent of the time they're normal size."

"Forty percent of the time midgets are normal size?" I repeated, then stared out over the ocean, considering how one simple truth can change the way you see the world.

My Grampy sat quiet with a bowl of soup, then mumbled "Some midgets are tall?"

My dad continued, "No, I mean their kids. Well, it's a major problem. I guess that a lot of little people's parents are regular size. That's not that big of a deal, but with couples where both people are midgets -- or maybe it was dwarves -- anyway something like forty percent of the time they have regular sized kids. Now you have to realize that these are people that have a very small lifestyle. Everything they do is small. They have little houses with little beds and chairs made especially for them. Suddenly they produce a regular size baby and it can't fit in the house anymore, they have to move and buy everything new."

While slurping soup, Grampy muttered, "Dwarves can be tall?"

"Maybe midgets, I'm not sure. Well, I think they were dwarves probably, are those the ones that have bigger feet? Is there another kind besides midgets and dwarves? Anyway, the point is their kids can't stand up in the house past eight years old, they go around breaking chairs and beds." My dad looked concerned.

So did Grampy, "These are violent midgets then? Wild little people with destruction on their mind. I saw a movie like that."

"Not violent, they just come out bigger than expected. It's a serious problem."

Grampy picked up the bowl to polish off the tomato soup. "Ahhh. Yup, short people in the movies. I like that guy from *Willow* too, he was very convincing. He really looked like he could've been one of those little people."

My dad cleared things up, "He's a dwarf, or some sort of challenged to be tall, how do you say it? Maybe a midget."

Grampy tapped the spoon at his empty bowl, a sign for someone to refill it. One of my aunts floated in and dropped a refill under his chin. Grampy looked deep into the tomato soup the way my dad considered the ocean. After a pause he looked up like he had found an insight, maybe a clue to the various distinctions of short people. "You know a lot of actors that you'd think are tall are actually really short."

"Maybe they just have short parents," I threw in.

"It's a serious problem for a lot of midgets, or the ones who have regular sized hands . . ." My dad stared off somewhere deep inside himself, or just beyond Grampy's soup.

Grampy continued, "There's one of those actors that I just found out is really short, but you would never know it."

I responded, "Oh, like Sylvester Stallone. He's tiny, but they make him look bigger by putting other actors in ditches, having him stand on crates. I saw a show on TV about that, it's a serious problem too. His parents were probably regular size and now his bed is too big for him."

"You should really watch that show," my dad admonished, "Then you'd understand the issues."

Grampy moaned. "No, no, not him. Not Stallone. It was a guy you would think is big, plays big roles. Umm, I can't think of his name."

"Well, what does he look like?" I started the questions off as others gathered around -- my family loves a good mystery.

Grampy shrugged his shoulders, "Kind of regular looking. Not one of those pretty boys but he's not bad looking."

My aunt rolled in and waved the rest of us off. "I know the perfect question. Would I think he's attractive?" She whispered to the rest of us, "He won't say if he thinks the guy is cute."

Grampy made a face like someone had dumped the soup on his head.

I jumped back in the round, "Alright Grampy, what kind of movies is he in. Comedies? Dramas?"

"This guy does it all. Serious, comedy, he can do everything."

"What kind of characters does he play, leading man, quirky side characters?"

"I'm telling you this guy could play me, your aunt Edye, he's a talent. And all without letting you know how short he is. He plays a lot of big characters, big stars, a real screen presence."

"Like Mel Gibson, right? He's short too, but he seems tall in his movies. Is he that kind of guy?"

"It's not him."

"Were his movies around the 70s, the 80s, or more recent?"

"Yup, he started early and he's still going strong."

"Is he in big Hollywood blockbusters, popular movies?"

"Absolutely, but he's not afraid to jump in a low budget picture if he likes the script."

Late into the evening we found out that the actor wasn't really that similar to Mel Gibson or Sly Stallone. He turned out to be Dustin Hoffman, just one in a long line of little actors that go to excessive lengths to hide their short stature, you know like Woody Allen or Tattoo from *Fantasy Island.*

My aunt looked displeased when Grampy finally remembered the actor's name. "Dustin Hoffman? More like Dustin Half-man. I thought he was a midget."

"I think the correct term is dwarf," my dad chimed in, "I saw a show the other day."

I began to wonder how big Dustin Hoffman's kids were.

Tactile Dome

My mom is a con-artist. Not a street thug or a corner hustler. Not a white collar thief, trading insider tips for stock options. She creates slippery solutions to household concerns, has scams for carpool lanes and YMCA memberships. She shows up with the friendly smile of a housewife on a peanut butter commercial, then leaves without paying library dues and parking tickets.

She is most well known for her mastery of the airport. She gets bumped from flights for free tickets, even when they weren't initially offering free tickets. She uses multiple check-in sites to send five boxes of stuff when one of her kids is moving across the country, taking pride in our family's history of moves with no shipping costs. One time the airline tried to charge us a fee for transporting a bike in a giant bike box. She borrowed their packing tape, stepped out of line and turned the bike box inside out. Returning to another line, we told them that this was a giant, flat box filled with clothes, just an odd sort of suitcase, and saved the fifty dollar fee.

My mom is cool under pressure, always says the right thing to security guards and talks her way out of speeding tickets. My dad is that friend that doesn't know the information on his fake ID, gets us all thrown out when the bartender asks him his birthday, gets kicked out of a movie that he paid for because he lost his stub. And my dad is always a reluctant participant in my mom's scams -- she throws him right in the middle and tells him not to speak.

My brother is named after my dad, so my mom takes advantage of combining their frequent flier mileage, especially as my brother began to fly more with his work. Then she'll try to use their built up miles to fly the rest of us around the country. Years ago, airport security was a little slack and my mom took full advantage. Several times, my dad had to check in and go to the gate, then return with a boarding pass for me to fly under his name. We were worried he would crack, sweat, respond to *How are you?* with *OK, I'm pulling a scam, stop interrogating me!* Once he was forced onto the plane because we were late, and the plane was about to take off. He would've been off to San Francisco in my place, a cheesy 80s movie where my dad returns to college and I'm forced to take over as a high school history teacher and track coach. He turned nervously to the stewardess, repeating *I have to ask my wife? I have to ask my wife?* He was escorted out to us by an airline agent, who my mom distracted while I grabbed the boarding pass and slipped on the plane in his place.

My parents come out to San Francisco to visit my brother and I as often as they can, flying mostly on legitimate tickets under their own names. We brought them to the Exploratorium, a science museum geared toward kids. My mom is now a high school biology and chemistry teacher, and loves the hands on approach of the Exploratorium. I had made reservations for the Tactile Dome, a sensory exhibit that involves crawling around through a dark maze. The Tactile Dome required reservations of about two months, so I made them for ten people and figured some of our friends would be around to join us.

Including my brother, my sister who was up from LA, my parents and some assorted friends, we ended up with a crowd of eleven that wanted to go to the Tactile Dome. "Don't tell your father," my mom said. "It'll just make him nervous. I'm sure we can sneak eleven in no problem." We arrived at the Exploratorium, and wandered around the exhibits for a while before our reservation. Little kids jumped to project shadows on the wall, built hairy faces out of shaved magnets, made giant bubbles, and watched chicks hatch from eggs. My mom loved it, it was perfect. Hands on science, little kids exploring, and a minor scam waiting in the wings.

My dad overheard us talking and said he was willing to sit out of the tactile dome, that he thought sneaking an extra person in was a bad idea. His offer was declined by my mom, despite my dad's protest that he would become the "laughing stock of the Exploratorium." This was a phrase he used often in our travels together, and claims that he has already been the "laughing stock" of Rome, Puerto Vallarta, American Airlines and the boyscouts.

Our time came and we entered a giant, honeycomb dome. We ducked under a low ceiling with billowing sheets, and entered a small carpeted room, with cubby holes along the wall and little signs everywhere. The signs had facts about nocturnal animals, pictures of ears and noses, and lots of rules of behavior. One little sign read: *Maximum number of people in the tubes: 20.* I saw a picture of a bat above a nose above a skinny board declaring: *No swearing in the tubes.* I turned to my dad, "Look. The bat knows(nose) there's no swearing in the tubes."

"Very funny." He pointed to an owl and then an ear. "The owl ears(hears) a bad joke."

A girl walked in wearing a beige collared shirt with many pockets, a possible heiress to the Panama Jack company. She was young, about twenty, with a ponytail, she looked cute but a little snotty. She stood behind a clipboard and rattled off a standard introduction, told us to take off our shoes and put them in the cubby holes, and warned us several times about bad language in "the tubes." I leaned over to my brother, "Watch your fuckin language in there." The girl and my dad scowled at me. Then she explained that the tubes we would be crawling through were connected to sound tubes that were projected throughout the museum, an interactive exhibit. And that people would be removed if they were disobeying the rules.

"Well, let's get started. The Tactile Dome is an interactive maze. You can crawl through as many times as you like in the forty-five minute period. Let's just check to make sure we're all here." She went down a list of names, "Johnson 4, Higaki 3, Carey 10."

"Yes," my mother replied. My dad raised a finger, contorted his face and was quickly pinched by my mom.

"Well, all of our groups are here." She counted the room. "We have a problem though. We have 20 reservations, and the maze can only hold 20 people at a time, and there are 21 people in the room right now. So who doesn't have a reservation here?"

The room was silent, my dad attempted to raise his hand and my mom pushed it back down to his side. We all figured the girl would give in if we could wait her out. All except my dad, who was probably starting to think he would be arrested.

"Who is not on the list?" She began to role call the groups again. "Johnson you have 4, Higaki 3, Carey 10." My mom nodded when our turn came.

"Well, even though the room is full of mostly adults, we'll have to get the individual list and see exactly who is here and who is not."

"I'm not on the list." My dad jumped up.

"And which group are you with?"

Possibly trying to save us, or deciding that he wanted out of this counterfeit family, my dad replied, "I'm not with any group."

"So you just came on your own, without any reservation, wandered in and took your shoes off?" She grew less cute and more snotty.

"Yeah, I guess so." My dad left the Tactile Dome, escorted, and with his shoes in hand.

Crawling through the tubes, we couldn't help talking about my dad getting thrown out, and his prediction of being the laughing stock of the Exploratorium. I eventually got thrown out a little early for saying something like, "I can't believe they fuckin kicked dad out."

I found my dad sitting outside the museum. "Sorry dad."

"I got kicked out in my socks, with no shoes on."

A guy was leaving the museum with his two kids, he must've heard some of our tube talk. "You're the laughing stock of the Exploratorium. Sorry man, I know how you feel. I'm the laughing stock of Pacbell Park. See ya later."

"See dad, that guy has it worse."

"He probably had his shoes on."

"Maybe he was streaking."

My mom wandered out, looked at my dad. "Honey, that was fantastic, you should've stayed with us. That's alright. I figured you'd get kicked out, but now I can use this as leverage for some free tickets to come back."

Misty's revenge

Pets in our house generally had a short life expectancy and a high turnover rate. We had a chameleon, turtles, a dog and of course countless goldfish. The chameleon got fried from too much time under the heat lamp. My dad would bring turtles home from the golf course. The largest one, which I named Wayne Newton, actually escaped form our backyard, perhaps the fastest and smartest turtle we ever had. Another small water turtle had drown in his bowl, and we found out later he was a land turtle. And everybody knows what happens to little kids' goldfish. I think that's where the expression a dime a dozen comes from. We had many a burial at sea, as we called them, and then flushed away the memories and thought of names for our next goldfish.

Most of the animals didn't fare too well under our care, even the temporary guests. My little sister Julie brought home the kindergarten class guinea pig, which rotated week to week among the students. Gretchen the guinea pig had an ugly little face and wasn't much for cuddling, but Julie loved her class mascot. My dad held firm to his idea that four little children were pets enough for one house, but with little effect. After a one day trial Michelle agreed to keep Gretchen for the week, with my mom's approval. After two days,

Gretchen started in with her high pitched middle of the night squealing. Over the next couple of days my dad was forced to take Gretchen to expensive vet visits and inject medicine down her throat, which needed to be done in the afternoon and at three in the morning. At the end of the week, Julie was informed that Gretchen couldn't be moved on until she had recovered from her illness. We endured another two weeks of midnight shrieks and howls, trapped in a bad horror movie -- *Attack of the Guinea Pig*, or maybe a documentary, a series of interviews with my dad called *Why Doesn't That Damn Thing Shut Up?*

One night the squealing deepened into a strange low roar, louder than before, followed by the dog growling and barking. We all came downstairs and the found the three of them frozen in the corner of the living room, Gretchen, the dog and my dad. Gretchen was really the most frozen of the three, laying on her back with her legs straight up in the air. Gretchen was wrapped in the newspaper she lay on, brought to the cellar, and put in the trash. Theories of the event were heated and diverse. One theory questioned whether the dog had given Gretchen a heart attack, or if the dog had arrived only as a consequence of Gretchen's death. This of course spawned a separate debate as to whether or not a guinea pig could have a heart attack. Another popular theory was that my dad had strangled the guinea pig in the middle of the night, the possibility of which gave most of us mixed feelings about my dad's behavior, somewhere between disgust and gratitude. Julie took it the hardest, sad for the loss of her pet and disdained by her classmates for the death of their mascot and the corrupt rumors that surrounded it. She came home in tears one day when a kid in class suggested she bring Gretchen's dead body in for show and tell.

The lone success of our revolving door animal shelter was our beloved dog Misty. Always in the background of our other pet tragedies, she was with us from the time I was born until I was fourteen. We all played with Misty, but she was clearly Julie's dog. Most of us fell somewhere between Julie and my dad in our feelings about the dog. Well, most people will find themselves somewhere within that scale, as the extremes on either side of them are scary. My dad was so blatant and consistent in his hatred of the dog, that we took his comments as jokes. We laughed along with jokes like, *I hate that dog*, and *someday I'm gonna kill that thing.*

Misty was a long-haired mutt, she looked sort of like Lassie but was much more dumb. Julie would brush her, whisper secrets into her big floppy ears, and take her on long walks. She spent hours trying to improve the dog food that we gave Misty. My parents bought giant bags of generic dry dog food. We used to measure ourselves against the bag. Oh look, I come up to the F in food now. The bag was white with large plain lettering: DOG FOOD. This was back when no-name brands were just that, white containers with black writing like props in cartoons.

Misty grew uninterested in her stale dry bulk chow, so Julie would try to garnish it up a bit. She would use spices, the way she saw my mom revitalize hamburger that was turning blue. Or she would add water to the dry food and mush it up with a fork. Julie tried to make it look like the food she saw on TV, which my parents explained was nicer steak than the kind we ate. I can attest to that with long hours of chewing steak at the table, and getting in trouble for not swallowing my food. Ray and I also spent time preparing the dog's food. We shared a strange fascination with trying to get the dog to eat grapes. Grapes were the only thing we had seen her completely refuse, and so we spent hours peeling, crushing, and hiding them in her food.

All of us played a lot with the dog. But while Julie spent most of her time cuddling Misty and trying to improve her care, Ray and I would try to break down her training and get her to do bad things. Our favorite game involved getting the dog into an excited state and encouraging her to break the house rules. Eventually, Michelle and even Julie couldn't resist and joined forces with us. We would stand in a circle around the dog, then slowly start our chants of *Mistymistymisty . . . mistymistymisty.* It was a rhythmic chant that grew louder and faster, and we clapped our hands on our thighs yelling *Mistymistymisty . . . mistymistymisty.* Misty would jump up on us and we'd keep her in the circle. We would get her into a frenzy, and then use her vulnerable state to coach her into behaviors she had learned to avoid. The big one was going upstairs. It was like experiments they used to do on children at university nursery schools -- let's spin them in circles and then tell them to go steal their grandfather's teeth. Misty would run upstairs or chew on my father's robe and the game was a success. Or we would work her into a sweat and then sneak a peanut butter covered grape her way.

Dog and man never developed a true friendship -- my dad and Misty scowled as they passed each other in the hallways.. Misty grew older and her wild fits were characterized by slow movements, and we all felt sad the day she finally gave in and ate a grape. When I was fourteen she was put to sleep, and about two months later we still had a half-filled bag of dry food left in the basement. My dad went down to the basement to get rid of the dog food bag. We gathered around as he struggled to pick up the bag. He slipped, swore and came out with a shoe covered in dog crap. We laughed.

My dad scratched behind his ear and sniffed the bottom of his shoe as we wondered how different he and Misty really were after all.

Lesbians

My dad has a plethora of childhood friends with funny names and stranger stories --- they usually enter conversations after questions that for most people would signify the end of a conversation, like *Who would actually cut off a toe for money?* or *Does anybody really have sex with those blow-up dolls?* My dad will often have several answers to these formerly rhetorical questions, and funny stories to go along with them. Most of the characters emerge from my dad's middle school days. A handful of these guys are now cops, and have busted a lot of the others over the years. We all remember a long conversation my dad had with a friend that was over for a visit, where they sat reminiscing, casually counting off the number of their classmates that were now either dead or in jail. And my dad was only in his mid-forties. Mikey Fitzbomb -- dead, Barry Schwabenfirst -- in jail, John Pinko died in jail, Harry Lipscumb -- dead, Ralph Finkle -- jail, Murray Stopher -- finally got out of jail, now he's dead. But mostly we heard stories of strange middle school kids pushing the boundaries of teenage hijinx – finding unexpected answers to conversation killers like *Why would you make bets on Pop-warner football?* and *Who would steal wine from the church?*

Out in San Francisco the closest I had come to this kind of crowd, outside of the daylight bar flies, was the dog park. I began to spend time at a dog park with my new female pit bull named Spartacus, after the sexual ambiguity of the classic gladiator film. (If you are unfamiliar, the best line is Tony Curtis' response to the question: *Do you like snails or oysters?* As he is being rubbed down in a Roman bath by a government man in a white sheet he turns and smiles, *I like snails and oysters.*) Spartacus has the harsh reputation that follows pit bulls, but is a playful female pup that attacks strangers only to lick their faces. She has the tough and tender sides of a well-oiled Kirk Douglas in S & M fetish wear, and they even share a little black dimple on their upper lip.

The dog park attracts a strange mix of owners, linked only by their pets and having little common ground outside of flea collars and the latest pooper scooper technologies. But the odd bunch brings forth interesting anecdotes. Many of the dog owners seem involved in some sort of oral tradition, spinning autobiographical tales that will have one owner fascinated and another disturbed. Most of them have been coming for years, and eagerly voice their concerns about newcomers.

I brought my dad to the dog park, hoping to use some of his stories as a sort of offering to the inner circle of regulars. The politics of the dog park are severe, and the formalities of discourse are often overtaken by verbal assaults – like British Parliament. We entered the park as one of the regulars hit the punchline of a dirty joke: "You gotta use douche. It gets the smell out." It turns out this was a home remedy for dogs covered in skunk spray. The young man who had brought the stench soaked dog was given a new technique and sent out of the park by the regular crew.

My dad and I fell to the side as Spartacus began to circle the regular crew with wild laps, chasing an ugly football sized dog with long hair and long teeth that hung over its lips at awkward angles. This was the little dirty mop of a dog I call

George Lucas, a sort of freaky futuristic sidekick with the look of a four legged ewok that got kicked in the face.

One of the new dog owners entered the park, the one legged guy with the three legged dog. The regular crew began a low grumbling, British Parliament coughing and moaning. Then one voice broke clear in a loud whisper, "I don't trust him." They were not extending the modern benefit of the doubt that goes along with a handicap. It seemed instead like some paranoid extension of the cinematic idea that bad guys have limps. But there was a logical reason. He continued, "We just don't know what order the loss of legs came in. Of course if he searched out the dog to match his own condition that's acceptable. But the morbid possibility of having a dog's leg removed to match your disposition, or the mental instability of removing your own leg in sympathy for a three legged companion . . ."

The skinniest member of the group bent down to play with the dirt. "I can't imagine any adult that would have a part of their body removed, just to match with something else."

A long pause left the crew to consider the idea of dismemberment as a show of sympathy, or an issue of matching. The circle of regulars tugged on their ears and scratched at their crotches, just a few butt sniffs away from the behavior of their pets around them. The shortest, largest man raised one hand while the other scratched his inner thigh feverishly. "What about circumcision?"

The skinny guy drew a phallus in the dirt and then sliced at it with a stick. "Cutting off the hood to match others. But not as an adult. Who in their right mind would get circumcised as an adult?"

A collective grumble was cut through by an outsider. "Franny Murphy." It was my dad. "Franny Murphy," he repeated as he sauntered his way toward the circle. "Then of course there was Larry Musto, at age 45, and he even did it himself."

Even Spartacus paused from her laps to consider this Franny Murphy and Larry Musto, brave men who had chosen a late stage of their lives to redesign their private parts. My dad entered the inner circle to provide details, and Spartacus locked him in with wild laps around the crew. Other dogs wandered over to join in the laps. I looked on from outside the dog track. As the inner circle grew more excited, Spartacus led a pack of dogs in feverish circles around the adult circumcision seminar.

Through the swarm of dogs, I caught a few bits of my dad's story, like "he sauntered up to Kelly's Roast Beef, very *gingerly*, and announced that he had gone ahead and done it to himself . . ." and "well, Murphy actually was supposed to have it done as a kid, but you know, you get busy . . . and thirty-two years later he looked down and didn't recognize his own penis." The inner circle seemed enthralled and overwhelmed. The skinny man stood up and the fat man sat in the dirt.

The dogs were suddenly quiet, and the fat man looked up from his seat in the dirt. "Hey, stranger. You there that knows so much about the men who circumcise themselves. Is that your dog? He's humping that rotwiler."

We all turned to see Spartacus grinding behind a big, smiling, female rotwiler. My dad looked down into the dirt, at the fat man. "That's my son's dog . . . but it's a girl. I don't know why she's humping that other dog?"

The skinny man bent down and helped the fat man to his feet. The fat man brushed off some dirt and addressed the inner circle, "Let me tell you about lesbians and dogs, and lesbian dogs."

After a long and strange lecture we gathered Spartacus and headed to the car. The inner circle welcomed my dad to membership in their crew any time he wanted. I remained outside the trust of the hardcore dog park guys, unknown and suspect like a one legged guy with a three legged dog.

I had hoped that a visit to the dog park would take the edge off of my dad's strange past, but realized that the experience had only made him stronger. He now had clever responses to conversation killers like *What else would you use douche for?* and *I wonder if some dogs are lesbians?*

Italy

Sometimes when you're with the same people for a week, they seem to develop a mantra or a phrase that becomes their contribution to the collective dialogue, like a squeeze-me toy with one line. My dad wandered the streets of Rome declaring, "In Italy, the wine is cheaper than the water." My mom spent most of her time pushing me toward crowds of disinterested locals, telling me to "talk Spanish to them." And my sister Julie, after one memorable afternoon, repeated the same line constantly like bad spanglish rap: "Mom, you put the mom in mamacita."

None of us had been to Rome before, but my dad took to walking backwards in front of us, pointing things out like a tour guide. "In Italy, my friends, the wine is actually cheaper than the water." We passed the Coliseum and he told us the history of the old gladiators, and pointed out some thirty of the hundreds of wild cats that lay stretched about the area. "People feed them like pigeons. Here in Rome the cat is king." I traced the behavior of kings to cats, and back to pigeons. I pictured Roman emperors picking at cannoli crumbs on the sidewalk, flying over the coliseum and shitting on the lazy cats beneath them.

A crowd of tourists gathered to watch a gang of young pickpockets try to rob another tourist. The youth were involved in an elaborate scheme, two of them bumping into the victim, then shuffling a wallet under a newspaper to a third member that handed it off to another. The tourist grabbed at the teenager with the newspaper, but the stolen wallet was already two streets away. The crowd jeered and then clapped. They laughed as the man impersonated a desperate tourist, robbed in plain sight of a crowd. One hand held firmly against their fanny packs, they reached for cameras while the gang surrounded their next victim.

My mom looked at me and back to the gang of pickpockets. "Why don't you go talk Spanish to them." None of us spoke Italian, and my mom was convinced that Italian and Spanish were a few slang terms apart. The second victim reached out for his wallet and the pickpockets, but caught only the newspaper. My sister snapped a picture. The man opened the newspaper and a string of pearls fell out. The crowd burst into hysterics and women chuckled as they clutched their jewelry.

"Let's keep moving," my dad suggested. He grabbed hold of a large fake leather purse that hung about his waist, his fanny pack. We called it the *power pouch* -- it was the size of a small back pack, built to hold cash and passports and trained to withstand the onslaught of Roman pickpockets we had read about in guide books. My dad wore his fanny pack in the front, driving it safely along the streets of Rome with two hands. We called it the power pouch for the way my dad respected it. That, and now that he wore it in front we couldn't think of any other names for it that my dad would approve of. The term fanny pack is a lot more acceptable than let's say, something like dick pack, nut sack, penis purse or crotch pocket, all of which were quickly shot down.

We wandered back toward our hotel. My dad gathered the tour together and raised one hand in his impersonation of an Italian waiter. "Ladies and gentleman, shall we visit our favorite local trattoria." He stretched the word trattoria like it had eight syllables. My dad loved the concept of the trattoria, little delis with tables in the back that offered restaurant quality meals at family prices, with a family atmosphere. My dad pointed inside and we headed into the same trattoria for the third time in four days. "Here my friends, you'll find that the wine is cheaper than the water." A glass of water in the trattoria cost about a dollar fifty, with quality glasses of Chianti available for a buck.

My dad liked the idea of repeat business, and the old men that littered the back room welcomed us with more excitement each time we returned. But mostly they loved my mom. She'd smile and wave. "Famile! Famile!" they shouted. Then my mom sent me to a dark corner to tell an old man in Spanish that she has eleven sisters. The old men shouted and gestured to my mom, "Bella! bella! We likah you bring you moma in."

The old guys had no interest in my thin, attractive sister. They clapped and shouted and my mom tapped her foot with a little dance move. "You moma too sexy, bella!" one of the old guys shouted. Then a deep voice muttered something from the corner and they all laughed.

The waiter came forth with garlic bread. "On the house, for you beautiful girl here." He winked at my mom. We had a long, delicious meal followed by complimentary slices of pie. "You come back see us," the waiter said. He looked at me, "You, who speak the Spanish, you bring you moma back for me." He winked. "Bring you moma later."

My dad shook his hand, "Thank you we will."

The waiter locked eyes with me, "You bring moma back."

The next morning we took a bus tour through the streets of Rome. Actually, my dad provided the tour as we road the public bus for several hours. My mom would later brag to her eleven sisters about finding the cheapest tour bus in Rome.

My mom called it "a tour of the real Rome" -- not those large air conditioned buses filled with old ladies; this bus was warm and stale and full of old Italian ladies.

My dad leaned up against a pole so he could keep two hands on the power pouch. I saw him swaggering to keep his balance and I put both my hands on a metal pipe overhead. Something slid gently into my pocket like a voluptuous Italian woman from travel brochures. I turned to flirt and found a skinny Italian man staring back at me. We looked down together at his hand in my back pocket and then back into each other's eyes. A few seconds passed before I made an extreme face and he removed his hand. The slim fellow slid to the back of the bus. Moments later I felt my wallet tremble and found him again with two fingers in my back pocket. This time I grabbed a hold of his hand, shook my head and waited for his shame. He took my disapproval as a sort of casual expression like *nice try*, or *oops, I caught you again*, and casually moved off.

After a few more miles and some excited discussion about my new pickpocket friend, we stumbled off the bus and into our little trattoria for lunch. "C'mon, it'll be fun. They already know us," my dad said. He paraded us in and smiled as the old guys stuck their tongues out and whistled at my mom.

"What do you have here that's cheaper than water?" my dad asked the waiter.

"Your wife, she good healthy girl."

"I'll have a glass of Chianti, then." My dad smiled.

This meal the waiter brought extra pizzas and pasta dishes, a feeding frenzy. They were fattening us for some American slaughter. Dinner was followed by shots of fruit liqueurs. Then one of the old men sang a song -- given the other guys' reactions, it seemed to be full of dirty jokes.

As we got up to leave, an old man came out of the shadowy corner to shake my dad's hand. "We likah you wife. She very nice." He turned to me. "We like you moma." Then he cupped his hands. "We like you mama's big round ass. You speaka Spanish, huh? You mama put the mama in mamacita."

Timeshare Scams

Growing up our exotic vacations were of a different sort, usually venturing from the Boston area into the lesser known regions of New Hampshire and Maine. We hit the unofficial, unsanctioned tourist locales. We would scour the highways for hand-painted cardboard signs leading to home-made theme parks -- free admission into somebody's back yard to see oddly shaped vegetables and six-toed cousins. Or sometimes we'd pay the fifty cents for a petting zoo full of diseased, unpredictable animals which you could normally find only in their domesticated state. These were the roadside hazards that AAA couldn't get the rights to. Photographs lie around our house of our more outlandish vacations. The more posh establishments had giant ceramic whales, or tall white men dressed as Indian chiefs. They were the Disneys of the northeast, full of politically offensive caricatures and looking like miniature golf courses.

But my parents were always on the lookout for something more, trying to find ways to stretch our budget. They rarely went out by themselves for dinner or a movie; usually a baby-sitter meant a visit to a timeshare or condo presentation, promising a free meal and maybe a family trip to the Poconos.

Our neighbor of about fourteen would watch the four of us, and we would torment her for several hours to make sure she earned the dollar fifty that was coming to her. On a night when one of us had threatened suicide or homicide, or had to be tied into bed with jump ropes, she could expect an extra quarter. My parents would return late bearing door prizes and stories about slide shows of far away lands. The house was full of imitation goods and shadows of deeper promises. The two main rewards for these presentations were usually luggage and cameras. Our dreams of exotic vacations were reduced to a pile of plasticky, purple suitcases and even cheaper cameras. My parents dreamed of China, but so far had only accumulated the relics of Chinatown.

I was in middle school when we had a chance to visit Florida, or as my little sister Julie called it Arflida. "I don't wanna go to Arflida," she pleaded with tears streaming down her face. "I wanna go to New Hampshire." My older sister tried to explain Mickey Mouse to her but she was unimpressed.

Having finally reached a tropical destination, our budget kept us searching out too good to be true deals and propositions. We waited several hours in a small hut by the airport for the cheapest deal on a rental car. Just before our rusty van pulled up, Julie passed out from the heat, and perhaps the excitement of Florida. So far this was more the Arflida that she had envisioned, and we all dreamed of New Hampshire.

We were joined on the trip by Paul Pruitt, who we all called Pruitt. He was a frequent baby-sitter and like an uncle to us, so when our trip plans came together for Florida we invited him along. Our destination was Disneyworld. We had a free place to stay, a family friend that lived two hours from Disney. We got up early the next morning, piled in the big, dented van and headed out. But with a family of six my parents were seeking out short cuts and deals. We exited the highway twenty miles before the Disney exit.

Florida has no shortage of schemers or condo scams, and we filed off to a presentation that promised free breakfast, only an hour of our time, and tickets for the family to Disney. My parents were carted away by a short man with big teeth that made sure they had brought their wallet and checkbook, and we were scurried off with Pruitt to the promised miniature golf course. We may not have been world travelers, but one of our vacation areas of expertise was certainly miniature golf. And we were old enough to tell the difference between a minigolf course and a sheet of plywood with carpet stapled to it, held up by bricks over a coffee mug. We hung around battling horse flies and hoping our parents had the same keen eye for lifting the astro turf and sniffing out a con.

The plan was an early morning breakfast at the timeshare thing, and onto Disney. It took about four and a half hours for my parents to convince the big teeth fella that they were broke, my mom finally using her checkbook to show their shriveled checking account and lack of savings. Somewhere around the fourth hour the big teeth had convinced them that they provided us with the promised meal -- we had shared a few ritz crackers and spray can cheese, although this was out of an old women's purse who was passing by and took pity on us. And somehow during the afternoon of meager snacks and alleged minigolf the words Disney tickets had become Disney discounts. It was late in the day when we finally left with our few bucks off Disney coupons. We were a couple of hours from our family friend, and so close to Disney -- but the park would be closing soon and Pruitt's mobility was limited by a belly full of spray can cheese.

My parents decided we would shack up in a cheap motel nearby and press onto Disney in the morning, first ones in and the last ones out. We hadn't planned on staying over, so my mom muscled her way into seven complimentary toothbrushes from the front desk, and extra towels. We all stripped down and turned our little motel room into a spa while my dad collected everyone's clothes to do a wash. What was to follow was an epic battle, a legendary stand-off between my dad and Pruitt that would entertain my family and my friends for years to come.

But first it's important to have a little background. Who was this Pruitt that tagged along on family vacations and knew volumes about minigolf and spray can cheese? He was Paul Pruitt, one of the Pruitt twins, both of whom were well known employees at Kelly's Roast Beef. Paul Pruitt, or Pruitt for our purposes, had a thick mustache and a thinning head of hair, and was known mostly for his Joe Cocker impersonation. John Pruitt, more commonly known as Bunga, had no facial hair and had shaved his head bald. He was widely known for his impersonation of a screaming line drive. Baseball players and enthusiasts for miles around swore that he could imitate the exact pitch and sound of a line drive baseball whistling by. This information may not seem to shed light on the nature and meaning of Pruitt's behavior in Florida, but at least you have some vague insight into what this Pruitt is all about. Oh yeah, and he was a bit of a sweaty, sop up all his plate and yours with an extra bit of bread, take showers when it suits him kind of guy.

We all relinquished our clothes to my dad, and arranged our towels into unique outfits that expressed our individual approach to white cotton. There had been some discussion about possibly venturing out for food. After several minutes of careful tucking and adjustments, we all looked about the same, sitting around a tiny motel room with white dresses and manly Tongan skirts. My dad in turn had reached Pruitt, who reluctantly gave up his clothes and adorned the last towel. My dad paused, turned back to Pruitt, "Let's have the rest." Pruitt tried to play it off with shrugs and jokes, but my dad held firm. He leaned over and gave a General's orders: "Give em up, let's go." Pruitt, a man in his thirties, about my dad's age, was not about to relinquish his personables without a fight.

Then my dad began a few minutes of an interrogating mantra, which has really encapsulated the moment, and has become a more sought after imitation than Bunga's screaming line drive. "Pruitt, give me your underwear." Or actually, as my dad phrased it in a thick Boston accent, "Pruitt, gimme youah undaweah." He repeatedly insisted, brushing off jokes, Joe Cocker lines and outright refusal, at one point adjusting his domineering stance to block Pruitt's exit. Where he would've fled to, in his white skirt and underwear we can't be quite sure. "Pruitt, gimme youah undaweah." We all stood around admiring the struggle, nodding in our tunics, like a meeting of the Roman Empire, or footage from old movies of arguments in heaven. "Pruitt, gimme youah undaweah!" And finally, he did.

The next day we did make it to Disney. By the time we left, we could hardly stand or smile, but we stayed until they closed the gate behind us.

✳✳✳✳✳✳✳✳✳✳✳✳✳✳✳✳✳✳✳✳✳✳

A pregnant woman walked over to our table and clasped her hands beneath her belly. "Hi, I'm Mary." We stopped eating and sat silent, trying not to look at her. She had on a summer dress covered with a pale ocean pattern. The way her belly protruded had a less comforting, tsunami feel to it. "Welcome," she offered in a cheerful squeal. "What a beautiful family. How are you folks?" I stared at scrambled eggs searching for an answer.

My older sister leaned over and whispered in my ear, "I bet she's not really pregnant."

We were on vacation in Mexico, in Puerto Vallarta, the exotic locale most referred to on *The Price is Right*. My younger sister was 24, I was 26, my older brother and sister 27 and 28. We were away as a family of six, well seven including my brother's friend Eric, who I think was 28 like Michelle. My parents had now traveled to China, Japan, Italy and been on safari in Africa. We had come so far in our vacation travel and experience. But how much had really changed? We wanted to venture out of town for the day, to some of the secluded beaches we had heard were a short drive up the coast. After walking by persistent corner booths for several days with no interest, the shouts of *honeymooners*, and *almost free* eventually seduced us like the call of the sirens. Somewhat interested in a promise of two free rental cars, we eventually sold ourselves for a free breakfast. We figured that we were going to eat breakfast anyway, and we would suffer a quick presentation while we ate, then be on our way in two free rental cars.

Now to understand our awkward silence in the face of a friendly young lady with a round belly, you have to understand the pre-war strategy talk that was given by my mom. Our basic plan was not to respond to questions, not show any interest, and therefore minimize our breakfast time and get out with the two rental cars while the sun was still threatening. "If they ask you anything, either say nothing, or tell them to ask your mother, in which case I'll say nothing. Trust me, I've been through this before." My dad would try to interject a note of something like we can still be friendly, and was quickly put back into rank by his commanding officer, mom. Now she turned my brother's friend. "Eric, we signed up for this as a family. So it's important that you tell them that you're our son."

Ray asked, "Do you really think they'll care if" --

One of my mom's eyes turned a cooler shade of blue. "Trust me, just follow my plan and we'll all get out. Individually we have no chance, but if we work as one unit we might just pull through this with a little waffles and bacon, and a car to get us to the sunshine. Stay focused."

Eric wasn't one of those neighborhood friends that grew up hanging around the kitchen and waiting for the bathroom with everyone else. He was my brother's friend from college, getting a quick introduction into life in this family, a fresh cadet thrown into action with little preparation. And he wasn't quite the type to usually hop into a family event. He was on the prowl, spring break mentality, cruising for babes with my family. He wore tight, fish-net club shirts out to dinner, soaked in musky cologne and adorned with a shark's tooth. My dad would comment, "Eric, I can see your nipples."

Eric would respond, as he often did, "Yeah, chics dig it." And then to my sisters, "Right girls."

He mistook their "Yeah sure" and giggles for approval, like when he bought the shark's tooth at the beach and checked with them to make sure that chicks would dig it. "Yeah, it'll hang between my nipples."

Here we were one big family, Eric with no shirt on at the breakfast buffet, collectively ignoring the friendly pregnant emissary they had sent to our table. "Having a fun vacation, kids?" We glanced at each other but made no contact with the "pregnant" voice. "How are you all?"

My mother made an unexpected chess move and prodded us to reply. "Kids, stop eating for a minute and say hello to this nice lady. . . Eric, dear, why don't you put your shirt on."

We glanced up and mumbled a few greetings. She had the face of a friend, but we knew she was the enemy.

"Well, these are all your kids huh, big family," She complimented

My dad spoke up. "Of course they're all our kids. Why wouldn't they be?" He was cracking, and a pinch under the table settled him down.

"Now, who's the oldest?" she asked.

An innocent question, but we hadn't prepared for it. We all looked up, a couple of us pointed to my older sister, a few to Eric, and we sat there frozen with our outstretched fingers pointing in different directions. My older sister jumped in, "Well, we're all very close in age," as if nobody was entirely sure what order we had come out in.

After a while the woman left, and as we were finishing our breakfast they brought in Harry, the closer. He ran from the back bullpen to finish off the last inning with strength. He gave us the old *hey, I'm an American knucklehead* speech - - you're not gonna believe the kind of deals these people are throwing around . . . just between you and me, I think they're making a big mistake . . . not the brightest business people . . . let's take advantage of the Mexicans . . . so you should really buy a timeshare today. My mom was not impressed. Harry reached far back from his training in Houston, Texas to try to reel in a big fish, as they had repeatedly told him in the workshops. Putting a miniature model of beachfront condos in Puerto Vallarta on our table, he asked my parents. "If this particular condominium with three bedrooms and fresh running water was free for you to use, one week out of the year for absolutely no cost, would you take it?"

My dad caved in, "Well sure."

Harry continued, "And do you think it looks like a place you would like to stay?"

"Yeah, it looks beautiful." I wiped my lip to try to tell my dad he had a hook in his mouth, to watch out for the slippery sales pitch.

Bright eyed Harry turned to my mom. "If it was free would you stay there?"

Without flinching, she tapped an orange peel like a cigarette and said, "No, I don't think so."

"Don't you think it's a nice, comfortable place to stay?" Harry engaged my mom.

"Nice, yeah. Comfortable, sure. But that's not really how we like to travel. We like to experience the real life of the places we visit."

My dad popped in. "Honey, we're staying at a Howard Johnson's right now." He was appropriately pinched and quieted down.

My mom continued, "We like to stay in places that are cultural, not comfortable."

My dad whispered to himself, "We could try a little more comfort."

"No, I definitely would not stay there for free. Fresh water," she scoffed. "It's not cultural and too comfortable."

A few minutes later we were on the road in two beat up metal sleds with lawn mower engines. They were called *Animals*, as they were certainly not cars. They appeared to have been driven right off of an amusement ride. After a beautiful afternoon at the beach, a heavy rainstorm began to assault the Animals, which had no real sides or windshield, and a little less roof protection than a golf cart. One of the Animals stalled out in a puddle. Eric took off his mesh shirt and tied it around the engine in an attempt to dry off the engine, and show the rural countryfolk his nipples. We abandoned the dead Animal and most of the family hitched a ride into town. I stayed behind with Eric and the other Animal, with my dad driving. As he was being beaten by rain, my dad threw out a rare couple of curse words, then followed them with a rainstorm of his own, a Tourette's roast of timeshare presentations and condo scams. "Fuckin mutha fucker ass shit fuck." My dad seemed to have a combination of poor decision making and short term memory, reliving the same epiphany after every timeshare scam. "This is the final word on those timeshare things. Shit ass fuck mutha fuck," he announced to the rain. "This is the last word on condo scams."

After our posh retreat at the Howard Johnson's in Puerto Vallarta, we took a bus to a small town to see my older sister's friend from Mexico. We stood up for several hours on the cheapest bus, cheapest out of six categories, together with crates of chickens and rotting fruit. If my mom wanted the experience that the chickens get bouncing around for hours in a large crate then we succeeded. As usual, my dad seemed to get the worst of it, sitting by himself among three mangey dogs that he was allergic to.

Michelle's friend and her family were welcoming. The house was located in a dry dusty region, littered with roosters and hot. Miami hot. Ball sweat hot. There was no shade, even in the house itself. The only breeze that came through was a tiny failing fan that blew through the kitchen, reaching little of the rest of the house. We left to see the town and hang out with my sister's buddy and her friends. My mom, of course, didn't want to miss out and came along. We left my dad home with Michelle's friend's dad, watching Spanish soap operas and soccer. Neither spoke a word of the other's language, and sat baking in the living room, smiling and nodding at each other. They did a little better with the soccer, as they could smile and nod more sincerely at the goals, which sadly only came about every half hour.

This went on for several days, and the heat was only rivaled by a general feeling of exhaustion, as sleeping there was like lying on fresh poured tar surrounded by noisy roosters. And they were too hot to crow right, or on time, screaming and cooing at random hours and pitches. One particularly oppressive afternoon, when we returned, one of the dad's was missing from the living room. We found my dad sprawled across the bed, in full view of the living room, Jesus-like with agony on his face and wearing nothing but his tighty whities. The roosters were laughing at him from outside, and one had ventured in to take a closer look at the seeming deceased. Michelle, embarrassed, tried to close the door over. My dad mustered what energy he had left through a dry mouth. "Coss bees. . . No, I need the cross breeze." My mother had gotten exactly what she wanted, a little suffering from my dad, and a vacation that was cultural, and certainly not comfortable.

Corn Muffin

"I'm not gonna laugh at a box." My mom stares blankly at the TV.

"But you think this show is funny?" I persist.

"Yup, very funny, but it's still just a box. It seems silly to me to laugh out loud at a box."

My mom has a strange sense of humor. She'll laugh out loud at a comedy show, but not a tape of it. Mostly she enjoys live theater, or reality theater, like watching my dad. Her favorite episodes are situations where my dad runs into a conflict or minor injury and then hilarious hijinx ensues. I have seen her sit quietly in the living room while others wail and moan at our small electric box. Sometimes boxes can be funny, maybe as a box of ice cream my dad forgot to put in the freezer, or a large box that he could trip over.

But I have never seen my mom more entertained than when she tells and retells the story of my dad and the corn muffin. It's like *The Little Match Girl* or *'Twas the Night Before Christmas*. We'll gather round the fire to hear yet another rendition of *Dad and the Corn Muffin*. I picture the children's book my mom will write. The cover has my dad looking off to the side, shaking his head, the frustrated straight man. His partner, the corn muffin, is a smiling Disney costume, a giant, bloated styrofoam muffin with skinny arms and legs poking out.

The story always takes a while to get going, as my mom bursts out lines in between fits of laughter. My parents are on the road, making good time to somewhere and living for the day off a bag of muffins and donuts. The supply is getting short and my dad's stomach growls. He looks to his stomach, then to my mom. "Honey, I'm hungry, should we stop somewhere to eat?"

"No, we've only got a couple more hours. Besides, we still have muffins left."

"Yeah, but all we have left is a corn muffin. I don't like corn muffins."

My mom rolls her eyes. "Of course you do. You eat corn bread. It's the same."

"I don't think so."

"If you squished corn bread into a muffin pan you'd get the same thing. You like it. Just eat it."

"I think I tried one the other day, and" –

"Just eat it. You don't know what you like."

At this point in the story, my mom usually has to take a quick break as narrator to catch her breath, laughing and coughing already before the story is really even underway. She calms herself and then continues. My mom rips the muffin in half, and gives him half. She breaks from the story, "I told him to eat it, and so he did; he took the corn muffin and had a bite of it." My mom is chuckling because my dad is doing what she suggested.

My dad will usually interject in this part of the story. "For some reason, your mother thinks it's hilarious that I trust her and take her advice."

My mom nods, cracking up and continues with the story.

My dad takes a bite and looks back at my mom like he was misled. "This muffin tastes bad. I don't like it."

"Honey, it's a corn muffin. That's what corn muffins taste like."

"It tastes gross," my dad protests.

"Don't be ridiculous, it's just because you want it to be blueberry. Just keep eating it, you'll get used to it. You like it, it's a corn muffin."

Now my mom can barely get the words out as she remembers the moments that followed. The hilarity builds for her before her audience has seen any cause for it. She focuses and stammers on. Then he takes another bite.

My dad is still unimpressed. "This muffin is disgusting. It tastes like cigarettes."

"Honey, now you're being crazy. Your imagination is taking over, that's what corn tastes like. Just eat it."

My dad takes another bite, and then another.

"So corn tastes like cigarettes?" my dad asks.

"You don't know what cigarettes taste like. The flavor you're tasting is corn." My mom shakes her head, "Cigarettes," and my parents share a moment, curling their upper lips at their hatred of cigarettes.

My dad takes one last bite, makes a dry gagging sound and spits something back into his hand. They stare together at a chewed up, corn-meal covered cigarette butt resting in his palm.

Through heavy breathing and now tears, my mom struggles to put forth the epilogue. Laughing hysterically, she considers the odds stacked against my dad. "The guy probably put one butt in a whole bucket of batter, and we get the one muffin . . . and dad gets the half of muffin with the butt in it."

My dad plays the straight man, shaking his head as family members join in the torture, calling him the *butt of that joke* and then calling that a *corny cigarette joke*.

The last page of the children's book has another picture of my dad with the corn muffin. His big styrofoam friend has a few bites out of him, but he's still smiling as he smokes a cigarette. My dad is next to him vomiting up something. In the background, along the horizon is a faint image of my mom bent over. Is she kneeling down, begging forgiveness? No, she's doubled over with laughter, holding her knees together and trying not to wet her pants.

USAA

My dad opened a letter, ripped it into pieces and threw it
away. Then he let out a short moan, dug through the trash
and began to make a puzzle on the kitchen counter. "I can't
believe this, our insurance company just dropped us. USAA
dropped our whole family policy. They can't do that, it's
illegal to drive without insurance in Massachusetts. I'm
calling them right now." He gathered the major pieces of the
letter and picked up the phone.

Our car insurance was through USAA, a company set up for
military personnel and their families, as a result of my dad's
years in the Air Force. I don't usually consider my family as
having a bad track record with driving. My mom drives out
of control, and considers the legal standards of driving as a
sort of annoying suggestion. But she has an incredible knack
for getting out of tickets, and an impeccable DMV record. I
was in the car when she was pulled over for speeding down
the wrong way of a one way street, with no shoes on. And
we were crawling around the bucket seats with no seatbelts
on, but I'm not sure if that was even illegal back then. The
cop seemed overwhelmed, and shocked by my mom's
insistence that he was holding her up and should get on with
it. Eventually he listed off eight or so possible infractions, and

the lengthy paperwork that would be involved. He was five minutes from the end of his shift and sent us on our way with no ticket, adding, "Your poor dad. Your poor dad."

Michelle was generally well behaved, and I don't think she has ever gotten in an accident or rolled through a stop sign. Julie has been in accidents, and gotten a couple of speeding tickets, but at the time of this phone call she was still driving in parking lots with my mom.

The men in the family have been the ones that left their mark on the auto insurance industry. I had a few early scratches with other cars and a couple of minor speeding infractions, followed by a totaled car on my parent's anniversary. But I guess my biggest achievement was totaling the family Volvo station wagon, a used banana yellow tank that seemed invincible. I crossed three lanes of traffic during a short nap on my way to St. John's, and woke as the car was being launched by the roadside guardrail, spinning and flipping along a patch of grass. The car landed on its side, and I crawled up to the passenger side door and slid out of the wreckage. A nearby construction worker ran over, and saw the underside of the yellow beast hissing steam. "It's gonna blow," he screamed, and we took off in slow motion away from the impending explosion. Minutes later we realized that we were not in a John Woo movie, and we wandered back to the hissing pile of yellow rubbage.

My parents took it very well. My dad was remarkably calm, having fallen asleep behind the wheel years earlier, driving home from an overnight shift at Kelly's and waking up in the middle of a tree. The station wagon was hauled off, and I escaped with minor injuries. A week later Ray fell asleep at a red light, and casually rolled into the back of a stopped Taxi. The damage was minor, but the cycle of sleeping male drivers was completed.

My dad held the phone away from his face like a microphone, screaming a passionate speech about the law and the purpose of insurance. The he took a deep breath and held the phone to his ear. The young USAA employee cleared his throat and said, "Mr. Carey, the average family of six in USAA over the last four years, has cost us approximately $1600 in auto claims. Your family, Mr. Carey, has cost us $109,000."

My dad said politely, "Thanks for your time," and turned his attention to us. Years later, all of my dad's children joined USAA auto insurance as a result of his time in the Air Force, though he has been permanently removed from their database.

(These are a few of the highlights, if not the complete story of my family's difficulty with auto insurance. Last year my brother was kicked out of USAA after Julie and I had both gotten into accidents in his car. They explained to him that his driving record was decent, but he should consider the type of characters he was lending his car to. At the time, I was still receiving a USAA good driver discount. I have since been banished from USAA. We continue to be one of the most feared father and sons teams in the auto insurance industry.)

The Brother-in-laws club

Going to see your girlfriend's family can be a difficult scene for anyone, but enduring a girlfriend with eleven sisters is the kind of scene that gets people screaming at the theater, *get out of the house*. Boyfriend visits to my mom's house had the slow, building tension of a psychological thriller. The girls could have easily and quickly used sheer strength and numbers to overtake the intruders. Instead they let the men take off their jackets and grow comfortable, and then slowly enveloped them in their madness like *The Fog* or *The Blob*.

My dad had the pleasure of dating the third oldest, way back in high school. Yes, that was my mom. Just because there's a dozen girls doesn't mean you just jump around to different family members. The only other male that wandered around that house at the time was their father, my Grampy. He worked two jobs, complete with weekend shifts, and was not to be disturbed in the rare moments when he had time alone in his study. Not to mention the sure exhaustion of so much procreating. My mom's sisters would find my dad and tell him that *Daddy* wanted to see him immediately in the study. After several minutes of standing awkwardly in the doorway, my dad would interrupt him. "You wanted to see me?"

"I don't want to see you." Sometimes Grampy would not look up at all, or look up without speaking, shooing away my dad like a fly that my aunts had sent in.

The girls repeated this game often, my dad never wanting to disappoint *Daddy* on the off chance that he did call for him, which never happened. Years later, having been formerly welcomed into the family by marriage, little had changed. Grampy appreciated my dad for providing the first grandsons, as he would talk of his dozen or so attempts at fathering a son. But the clan of girls, many of whom now had their own man to torture, continued with their collective games. Like spiders they waited until their boyfriend or husband had entangled himself fully into their family, and then surrounded and devoured him. A typical con would involve watching a beloved one panic over a story of fake tragedy and then revealing the mischief. Perhaps years later a boyfriend would look back and chuckle, remembering the day he thought that his dog was run over or his best friend was sleeping with his girlfriend.

The more involved pranks were reserved for the husbands, the brother-in-laws, who by their sworn commitment were less likely to consider revenge or seek legal assistance. The standard hazing that many had undergone included the old dog food gag. This was a tray of hors d'oeuvres featuring ritz crackers covered with dog food. The effect was sealed with moving performances by several of the sisters eating similar looking, non-dog-food hors d'oeuvres.

A few of the husbands banded together, trying to appear unafraid of the gaggle of sisters around them. They declared themselves the Brother-in-laws Club, embracing the trauma that now defined their lives. Cigars and matching Hawaiian shirts provided a thin, translucent coat of protection against the power of the unified sisters. My dad was an outspoken dissident among the brother-in-laws core. His bold refusal to join only increased their interest in him, convinced that he represented the kind of unbridled individualism they could unite behind.

One afternoon at my grandparents house, a dog biscuit tray had already made its appearance in honor of my aunt Renee's new boyfriend, Sonny. Afraid that joining forces was his only chance to escape, he ate several and declared that he loved dog food. Later, he hid outside beneath large cop sunglasses, trying to avoid the excitement that his visit had developed into. We were playing ball in the yard, and my dad was wandering about the kitchen observing the plotting girls. The Brother-in-laws Club was trying to squeeze information out of my dad, who because of his outspoken denouncement of the Brother-in-laws Club was the only male allowed in the kitchen. He was like Switzerland. The brother-in-laws caught up with him in their red, matching Hawaiian shirts and cigars. They tried to bribe him with chocolates. Switzerland has no need for chocolates.

The brother-in-laws rolled outside, a pile of red tropical trees and birds, spitting cigar smoke. They found Sonny sitting outside with no shirt on, peering out behind huge sunglasses and chewing on dog biscuits. They considered dressing him up with a red pineapple shirt, to blend into the rolling red menace of Chalifour girl accessories -- the Brother-in-laws Club. With this drastic move to incorporate a non-married into their ranks, they felt my dad would have no choice but to cave in and wear luau shirts to family reunions. They were using Sonny as bait to catch the great dissenter, my dad. Something infiltrated their gathering in the heat of discussion, pushing it's way through the crowd and onto Sonny's face. A water balloon from the balcony of the house had broken through Sonny's glasses, which cut his cheek. It was difficult for Sonny to play this one off, claiming that he loved cuts on his face and giving himself a few more.

Several minutes passed in a Sherlock Holmes type finale as the brother-in-laws gathered evidence and collected the suspects. Nobody would admit to throwing the balloon, and all of the sisters had been nearby but suspiciously saw nothing. My dad walked forward and said simply, "Renee did it. I saw her do it." As he headed away my dad was quickly enveloped in a sea of red flowers, papayas, and pineapples. One of my uncles ripped a box open and presented my dad with a red shirt and a cigar. Renee rushed over to Sonny, who held a block of ice to his eye and chewed a dog biscuit. "Sorry about that," she said. "Now clean yourself up, Daddy wants to see you in his office."

Printed in the United States
21566LVS00002B/1-24